Praise for *Murder in Amsterdam*

"*Murder in Amsterdam* is indispensable. Buruma delivers the most fruitful insights on the 'clash' between the East and West today. Why? Because he finds connections and complexity where most observers only see an irreconcilable conflict." —*San Francisco Chronicle*

"Ian Buruma addresses questions of political philosophy, moral accountability and mass psychology in the most rigorous possible way: journalistically. . . . He has deftly combined interviewing and reflection. This proves a fruitful way to approach the murder, in 2004, of the filmmaker Theo van Gogh." —*The New York Times Book Review*

"Mr. Buruma is such a good writer and reporter that *Murder in Amsterdam* is always engaging." —*The Wall Street Journal*

"Splendid." —*The Economist*

"This is a masterful ensemble piece, a tragedy of tolerance, in which characters drawn with quick, precise brushstrokes get caught in the same lethal gravity, leading to the murder of filmmaker Theo van Gogh." —*New York*

"[An] intrepid reporter and gifted stylist . . . Buruma packs the high drama and raw suspense of an intellectual thriller into this revelatory book, which elucidates how profound and age-old antagonisms are testing anew the sometimes sharply conflicting premises and practices of modern Western societies—particularly as they relate to women, minorities, and differing faiths." —*Elle*

"[*Murder in Amsterdam*] is a work of philosophical and narrative tension, strikingly sharp and brooding, frank and openly curious. Which is apt, for here is the Netherlands—home to the Enlightenment, bastion of tolerance—experiencing an act of mortal intolerance." —*San Francisco Chronicle*

"Buruma is one of the planet's wisest heads and best writers about the politics of national identity, civilization, and culture. With the eye of a novelist and the erudition of a scholar, he finds in the frenzy of soccer fans no less than in the history of the last several centuries an explanation for the violence that has erupted in the land of Rembrandt and tulips. This is a book about much more than a single crime in a single city. It is a brilliant insight into what ails Europe and, more broadly, our globalized world." —Strobe Talbott, president, Brookings Institution

"Buruma . . . is in a unique position to explain Holland's predicament to an English-speaking audience, and his slim but free-ranging investigation succeeds, in part, because he's willing to wrestle with the larger issues raised by Van Gogh's death. . . . Buruma's greatest virtue is that he understands the ways in which site-specific tensions in Holland tie into larger historical currents, and he is as good at describing those currents as he is at picking out details . . . that drive his arguments home."

—*Bookforum*

"Ian Buruma is surely one of the finest literary journalists at work today. In *Murder in Amsterdam,* he delivers a searching and brilliant meditation on Holland's—and by extension much of the West's—encounter with Islam. With great care, he dissects the interaction of Dutch culture, with its paternalistic tolerance and xenophobic nostalgia, with the alienation and cultural traditionalism of Muslim immigrants. It is a deeply humane and troubling book on a subject that will be with us for a long time—not the last book on the subject, but the one that will inform all that follows."   —Daniel Benjamin, coauthor of *The Age of Sacred Terror* and *The Next Attack*

"Buruma is refreshingly direct. . . . He convincingly dissects [Holland's] reluctance to recognize the dangers within its borders. . . . Rather than using Van Gogh's murder as an occasion to pillory Dutch tolerance or radical Muslim intolerance, Buruma probes the psychological world of unassimilated 'outsiders' who are caught between a homeland that couldn't sustain them and a new one that can't fully embrace them."

—*BookPage*

"I heartily recommend Buruma's book. He has written a vivid account that is both serious and witty, and cuts through the clichés about multiculturalism. This book is not just about the murder of Van Gogh in Holland; it is about the nature of Islam in Europe, and, by extension, about the soul-searching quest among the Europeans themselves for a European identity."   —Olivier Roy, author of *Globalized Islam*

"Ian Buruma's *Murder in Amsterdam* provides the reader with an extraordinary understanding of the dramatic change in European societies in the age of multiculturalism. The murder of filmmaker Theo van Gogh by a young Dutch Moroccan turned jihadist is investigated thoroughly, with a deep and firsthand knowledge of the Netherlands, and reveals the challenges faced by immigrant Muslim and native European cultures as they have to accommodate to each other, whether to blend or clash. Buruma's subtle book is an eye-opener."

—Gilles Kepel, author of *The War for Muslim Minds*

PENGUIN BOOKS

MURDER IN AMSTERDAM

Ian Buruma is currently the Luce Professor at Bard College. His previous books include *God's Dust, Behind the Mask, The Missionary and the Libertine, Playing the Game, The Wages of Guilt, Anglomania,* and *Bad Elements.*

Murder
in
Amsterdam

Liberal Europe,

Islam

and the

Limits of Tolerance

IAN BURUMA

PENGUIN BOOKS

PENGUIN BOOKS
Published by the Penguin Group
Penguin Group (USA) Inc., 375 Hudson Street, New York, New York 10014, U.S.A.
Penguin Group (Canada), 90 Eglinton Avenue East, Suite 700, Toronto,
Ontario, Canada M4P 2Y3 (a division of Pearson Penguin Canada Inc.)
Penguin Books Ltd, 80 Strand, London WC2R 0RL, England
Penguin Ireland, 25 St Stephen's Green, Dublin 2, Ireland
(a division of Penguin Books Ltd)
Penguin Group (Australia), 250 Camberwell Road, Camberwell,
Victoria 3124, Australia (a division of Pearson Australia Group Pty Ltd)
Penguin Books India Pvt Ltd, 11 Community Centre,
Panchsheel Park, New Delhi – 110 017, India
Penguin Group (NZ), 67 Apollo Drive, Rosedale, North Shore, Auckland 0745,
New Zealand (a division of Pearson New Zealand Ltd)
Penguin Books (South Africa) (Pty) Ltd, 24 Sturdee Avenue,
Rosebank, Johannesburg 2196, South Africa

Penguin Books Ltd, Registered Offices:
80 Strand, London WC2R 0RL, England

First published in the United States of America by The Penguin Press,
a member of Penguin Group (USA) Inc. 2006
Published in Penguin Books 2007

1 3 5 7 9 10 8 6 4 2

THE LIBRARY OF CONGRESS HAS CATALOGED
THE HARDCOVER EDITION AS FOLLOWS:
Buruma, Ian.
Murder in Amsterdam : the death of Theo van Gogh and
the limits of tolerance / Ian Buruma.
p. cm.
Includes index.
ISBN 1-59420-108-0 (hc.)
ISBN 978-0-14-311236-5 (pbk.)
1. Gogh, Theo van—Assassination.   2. Netherlands—Ethnic relations.
3. Europe—Ethnic relations.   4. Toleration—Netherlands—History—21st century.
5. Toleration—Europe—History—21st century.   I. Title.
DJ91.B87   2006
364.152'40892—dc22   2006043606

Printed in the United States of America
Designed by Stephanie Huntwork

For Hanca

Contents

ONE

Holy War in Amsterdam

1.

Ton (48), eyewitness to the murder of Theo van Gogh on November 2, 2004: "I heard Theo van Gogh beg for mercy. 'Don't do it! Don't do it!' he cried. I saw him fall onto the bicycle path. His killer was so calm. That really shocked me. How you can murder a person in such cold blood, right there in the street?

"I had sleepless nights for weeks. . . . Every night I see Theo van Gogh fall and Mohammed B. quietly finishing his job. . . . Since then I trust very few people. Mohammed B. could be one's neighbor. If I say 'fucking nigger' to a Surinamese, I'm called a racist, even though he can call me a whitey. You can no longer say what you think these days. No, we've become foreigners in our own country."

NRC HANDELSBLAD, JULY 30, 2005

It was the coolness of his manner, the composure of a person who knew precisely what he was doing, that struck those who saw Mohammed Bouyeri, a twenty-six-year-old Moroccan-Dutchman in a gray raincoat and prayer hat, blast the filmmaker Theo van Gogh off his bicycle on a dreary morning in Amsterdam. He shot him calmly in the stomach, and after the victim had staggered to the other side of the street, shot him several more times, pulled out a curved machete, and cut his throat—"as though slashing a tire," according to one witness.

Leaving the machete planted firmly in Van Gogh's chest, he then pulled a smaller knife from a bag, scribbled something on a piece of paper, folded the letter neatly, and pinned it to the body with this second knife.

Van Gogh, a short fat man with blond curls, was dressed in his usual T-shirt and suspenders. Most people in Holland who watch TV or read the papers would have been familiar with this ubiquitous figure, known less for his films than for his provocative statements on radio and television, in newspaper and Internet columns, and in various courts of law, about everything from the alleged exploitation of the Holocaust by Jewish celebrities to the dangerous presence of a Muslim "fifth column" operating in Dutch society. He lay on his back, his hands stretched above his head, two knives sticking out from his chest, slaughtered like a sacrificial animal. Bouyeri gave the corpse a few hard kicks and walked away, without hurry, easy as could be, as though he had done nothing more dramatic than fillet a fish.

Still calm, he made no serious attempt to escape. While he reloaded his gun, a woman who happened by screamed: "You can't do that!" "Yes, I can," Bouyeri replied, before strolling into a nearby park with several patrol cars rushing to the scene, "and now you know what you people can expect in the future." A shootout began. One bullet struck a policeman in his bulletproof vest. Another hit a passer-by in the leg. But then Bouyeri caught a police bullet in his own leg and was arrested. This was not part of the plan. Bouyeri had wanted to die as a martyr to his faith. We know this from statements he made later, and from the letter on Van Gogh's chest.

The content of Bouyeri's letter was not released to the public for several days. Perhaps it was thought to be too shocking, and likely to provoke further violence. It was in fact a long rambling tract, written in Dutch with a few quotations in Arabic, calling for a holy war against the unbelievers, and the deaths of a number of people mentioned by name. The tone was that of a death cult, composed in a language dripping with the imaginary blood of infidels and holy martyrs. The Dutch is correct but stilted, evidence of the author's lack of literary skill perhaps, but also of several layers of awkward translation. Much of Bouyeri's knowledge of radical Islamist rhetoric came from English translations of Arabic texts downloaded from the Internet.

The manner of Van Gogh's murder, too, appears to have been inspired by imagery shooting around the world on websites. A CD-ROM disk was found in Bouyeri's apartment with video film of more than twenty-three killings of "the enemies of Allah," including the American reporter Daniel Pearl. These were taken from a Saudi website edited in London. Apart from the detailed images of men of various nationalities being beheaded, the CD contained pictures of a struggling man slowly having his head sawed off, taken from a Dutch porno site.

Bouyeri's "open letter" was not actually addressed to Theo van Gogh himself, but to Ayaan Hirsi Ali, the Somali-born Dutch politician, who had made a short film with Van Gogh, entitled *Submission,* dramatizing what she saw as Islamic abuse of women by projecting quotations from the Koran onto the naked bodies of several young women. The film was first shown in a television program in which Dutch celebrities are asked to select scenes from their favorite films or television shows. Hirsi Ali chose *Submission.* Selecting one's own work was unusual, perhaps even unprecedented, but Hirsi Ali was not a run-of-the-mill celebrity. In the year before Van Gogh's murder she had become the most prominent critic of Islam in the Netherlands, speaking out in meetings with Muslim women, at party conferences, and on TV talk shows, repeating her message, over and over, that the Koran itself was the source of violent abuse. A delicate African beauty, Hirsi Ali had caught the public imagination by the eloquence and conviction of her public warnings against a religion which already had a sinister reputation. Here was a Muslim, or ex-Muslim, from Africa, telling Europeans that Islam was a serious threat. This was a disturbing message in a society used to public figures preaching multicultural tolerance, but it was also something many people wished to hear, some of the same people who would later turn against her.

Bouyeri's letter was addressed to Hirsi Ali, as a heretic who had rebelled against her childhood faith and become a willing tool of "Zionists and Crusaders." She was called a "soldier of evil" who had "turned her back on the Truth." She was "a liar" who would "smash herself to pieces on Islam." She would be destroyed, along with the United States, Europe, and Holland. For death would "separate Truth from lies," and Islam would be "victorious through the blood of martyrs."

Ayaan Hirsi Ali was the most prominent target of this holy rage, but she was not the only one. Her "masters" were described in the letter as a Jewish cabal that ruled the Netherlands. This cabal included the mayor of Amsterdam, Job Cohen, a secular man who actually tried his best to find common ground with the Muslim communities in his city ("holding things together," as he put it). In a twist of awful irony, Cohen had also been attacked quite viciously by Theo van Gogh, among others, as an appeaser of Islamic extremism.

The shadow of World War II, the only war to reach the Dutch homeland since Napoleon's invasion, is never far from any Dutch crisis. Van Gogh, with his unfailing instinct for the low blow, compared Cohen to a collaborationist mayor under Nazi occupation. Still, in Bouyeri's jihad, Cohen would have to be annihilated. Another member of the alleged cabal was Jozua van Aartsen, then leader of the conservative VVD,* People's Party for Freedom and Democracy, which Hirsi Ali had recently joined as a member of parliament. The fact that he wasn't Jewish at all was of course irrelevant. In the holy war against "Zionists and Crusaders," ancestry counts for less than association.

Van Aartsen, too, invoked the last war. "These people," he wrote in the *NRC Handelsblad*, the most august of the national newspapers, "don't wish to change our society, they want to *destroy* it. We are their enemy, something we have not seen since 1940." His party colleague, the finance minister, Gerrit Zalm, a personal friend of Van Gogh's, declared that "we" were "at war" with the terrorists, and extra measures would be taken "on all fronts." Matt Herben, leader of the populist LPF** party, founded by the late Pim Fortuyn,

*Volkspartij voor Vrijheid en Democratie
**Lijst Pim Fortuyn, or Pim Fortuyn's List

saw Islamic and Western civilizations at war on Dutch soil. Society, he said, "is being threatened by extremists who spit on our culture. They don't even speak our language and walk around in funny dresses. They are a fifth column. Theo said this better than anyone."

First it was a mosque in Huizen—three men tried to torch it with turpentine and gasoline. Then a mosque in Rotterdam was targeted, though only the door got scorched. There was another arson attempt at a mosque in Groningen. And in Eindhoven a bomb exploded in an Islamic school. Jan Peter Balkenende, the prime minister, quickly announced that "we" were not exactly at war; Holland was just "doing battle" against "radicalism." Three Christian churches were attacked, in Rotterdam, Utrecht, and Amersfoort. Another Muslim school, in Uden, a small town in the south, was set on fire. Someone had written "Theo R.I.P." on the wall. "The country is burning," said the announcer on the television news.

In fact, the country wasn't burning at all. The arsonists in Uden were a bunch of teenagers looking for kicks. The "civil war" that some feared, the pogroms on Muslim areas, the retaliations by newly recruited jihadis, none of this actually happened. Most people kept their cool. But the constant chatter of politicians, newspaper columnists, television pundits, headline writers, and editorialists in the popular press produced a feverish atmosphere in which the smallest incident, the slightest faux pas, would spark endless rounds of overheated commentary.

An orthodox imam from Tilburg refused to shake the hand of Rita Verdonk, minister for the integration of minorities. With all respect, the Syrian-born cleric said in halting Dutch, she was a woman, and his religion forbade physical contact with strange women. "But surely we are equals," replied Verdonk a little peevishly, unsure what to do with her outstretched hand. She was right, they were equals, but equality may not have been the point. The imam's refusal, maladroit no doubt, but not of huge significance, made the front page of every major newspaper. The sturdy figure of Rita Verdonk facing the bearded imam became a prime symbol of the Dutch crisis, of the collapse of multiculturalism, the end of a sweet dream of tolerance and light in the most progressive little enclave of Europe.

2.

Forty Moroccan, Dutch, political, religious, and homosexual organizations from Amsterdam distributed posters with the slogan: "We won't take this." People are invited to sign a manifesto on the website www.wewonttakethis.

NRC HANDELSBLAD, NOVEMBER 16, 2004

It was at this point that I decided to spend some time in the Netherlands, where I was born in 1951 and had lived until 1975. I had known Van Gogh slightly. We had mutual friends and did the odd radio show together. He invited me to be on his TV talk show, called *A Friendly Conversation*, which, in fact, it was. Not being a member of Amsterdam café society or the local literary scene, I had escaped the lash of his often venomous polemics. His behavior to me was invariably polite, even though his loud, high-pitched voice, always striving to be heard, could be wearisome.

I arrived with an American magazine assignment in time for Verdonk's attempted handshake, but too late for the memorial party organized by "the Friends of Theo" according to the precise specifications of Van Gogh himself, drawn up while planning a trip to New York a few months earlier (he suffered from a fear of flying). There was a rock band and there were cabaret acts. Pretty cigarette girls in miniskirts plied their wares, as in a prewar movie theater. Female guests wore strings of pearls and twinsets, a style that Theo had found a turn-on. Since one of Theo's favorite terms for Muslims was "goat fuckers," well-known comedians made jokes about fucking goats, and two stuffed goats stood on a makeshift stage, ready for "those who might feel the urge." A large wooden coffin, supposedly containing Theo's corpse, was placed on a revolving platform flanked by magnum bottles of champagne, and large phallic cacti, the trademark of his television chat show. One Friend of Theo, present at this wake for a more frivolous age, predicted to me that if the Muslim radicals weren't crushed soon, there would be a civil war in Holland.

There was something unhinged about the Netherlands in the winter of 2004, and I wanted to understand it better. Hysteria, after all, is the last thing people associate with a country that is usually described by lazy foreign journalists as "phlegmatic." I had always known this to be a caricature, but had still found it too placid for my taste, too reassuringly dull. This, clearly, was no longer the case. Something had changed dramatically in the country of my birth.

One of the first things I read after arriving in Amsterdam was an essay by the great Dutch scholar Johan Huizinga, written in 1934, another time of crisis, when fascism and Nazism were looming close to the Dutch borders. But extremism would not seduce the Dutch, he said, and even if it did, against all the odds, it would surely be a "moderate extremism." Even though Holland was not immune to the dangers of modern propaganda and the crumbling of faith in democratic institutions, the stolid Dutch burghers were simply not given to excesses. As Huizinga saw it, the "mental basis" for collective illusions was a "political sense of inferiority" grounded in centuries of failure and oppression, and a deeply felt loss of ancient glory. Exasperated nationalism is the usual result, filled with a desire for revenge. Such was not the case in the Netherlands, for "as a nation and a state we are after all *satisfait,* and it is our duty to remain so."

Huizinga's view on the national character, though not exactly wrong, did reveal a certain complacency. Bourgeois satisfaction is by no means to be despised; indeed, it is a recipe for peace and orderly contentment. It is also, perhaps, a trifle boring. Heinrich Heine did not mean it as a compliment when he said that he would head for Holland when the end of the world was in sight, since everything in that country happened fifty years later. Like most quips of this sort, it was unfair, yet not totally untrue, especially in the nineteenth century. By the middle of the twentieth century, however, the Netherlands had pretty much caught up with the world, and since then things often happened earlier than elsewhere: tolerance of recreational drugs and pornography; acceptance of gay rights, multiculturalism, euthanasia, and so on. This, too, led to an air of satisfaction, even smugness, a self-congratulatory notion of living in the finest, freest, most progressive, most decent, most perfectly evolved playground of multicultural utopianism.

I had left Amsterdam in the winter of 1975, at the height of its good times, driven by a traditional Dutch wanderlust, a desire to set sail for the wider, larger world, but also by a certain boredom with the Dutch idyll. My restlessness may well have been a sign of growing up in a pampered society, where there was always enough to eat, and no one had to fear a knock on the door after midnight. Yet there were cracks showing in the national idyll even then, as I was leaving. Seven young Moluccan activists had just seized a train in a province near the German border and held the passengers hostage in an attempt to get Dutch support for the independence of the south Moluccan islands from Indonesia. When the hijackers failed to get their way, the engine driver and two passengers were murdered and, to the horror of millions watching TV, tossed casually onto the tracks. On my way to the airport, we had to make a detour because the Indonesian consulate had been occupied by Moluccan activists shooting off guns.

These acts of violence, or terrorism, have been largely forgotten now. There were no heroes in this story, and the villains were more pathetic than monstrous. It was in fact a typical case of unresolved colonial bad faith. Moluccans, many of them Christians, had fought on the Dutch side in colonial wars. Like minorities in other European empires— the Hmong in Indochina, the Indian Sikhs—they served in colonial armies in exchange for privileges and protection. When the Japanese invaded the Dutch East Indies in 1941, the Moluccans—unlike most Javanese—resisted on behalf of the Dutch, and were treated by the Japanese with special venom. When Indonesia declared independence after the

Japanese defeat, the Moluccans once again fought alongside Dutch troops, in a brutal campaign ("police actions") to crush the Javanese-led independence movement. It was a bloody as well as a hopeless cause.

The Dutch finally left Indonesia in 1949, and they took the Moluccan soldiers with them. They had no choice, since the Indonesians would not let the "traitors" go home to the Moluccas. But since the Moluccans had no desire to rebuild their lives in the cold and frowsy towns of postwar Holland, and the Dutch had no desire to let them stay, the Moluccans were promised a swift return to an independent homeland. The Dutch would see to that. But of course the Dutch had no intention of creating any more trouble with Indonesia. So the poor Moluccans were shunted off to former Nazi concentration camps, such as Westerbork, from where, less than a decade before, almost a hundred thousand Dutch Jews had been deported, most never to return. Westerbork had been built originally for Jewish refugees from Nazi Germany in the 1930s. That, too, was supposed to have been a temporary solution. They, too, were not expected to stay. By 1975, it was clear that independence for the south Moluccans was an illusion, a deceitful promise of a false dawn. A new generation had grown up with no hope of returning and no life outside the camps. It was not a good start to the new age of multiculturalism.

3.

Amsterdam, December 21: The family of the murdered film-maker Theo van Gogh is angry with Prime Minister Balkenende for his failure to console the next of kin. The Government Information Agency denied this. Yesterday night in the television program Nova, *Van Gogh's mother reproached the prime minister for . . . visiting a mosque as well as an Islamic school, while forgetting about a little boy whose father had been murdered in Amsterdam.*

NRC HANDELSBLAD, DECEMBER 21, 2004

Immediately after Van Gogh's murder, the bickering began. Within hours, shock curdled into recrimination. Ministers in The Hague blamed the AIVD, the domestic intelligence service, for its failure to keep a closer eye on Mohammed Bouyeri. The prime minister and the minister of justice were blamed for not tackling hate speech in the mosques. Job Cohen, the Amsterdam mayor, blamed the AIVD for not sharing intelligence with the Amsterdam police. The interior minister, in charge of the AIVD, was blamed for letting terrorists roam free. Ayaan Hirsi Ali was blamed for causing unnecessary offense with her polemical film. Theo van Gogh was blamed for insulting the Muslims. The Friends of Theo, a select band of quotable voices in the national and international press, blamed Cohen for being a coward, the government for being careless, the Muslims for being in denial, the prime minister for being unfeeling, and the Netherlands for being a miserable little country that let one of its geniuses die. And the Friends of Theo were accused in turn of being "merchants of fear." The real rot, yet others opined, set in with a generation of arrogant Social Democrats who had failed to see the emerging "drama of multiculturalism" and denounced those who did as racists.

This is the other side of complacency, of being a little too *satisfait*. When smugness is challenged, panic sets in. There was in the finger-pointing a tone of wounded *amour propre*, of resentment that things had suddenly gone wrong, a sense of pique, of being affronted by one's own shattered dreams. There is a Dutch word that perfectly expresses this feeling: *verongelijktheid,* to be wronged, not by an individual so much as by the world at large. You could see it in the faces of people who turned up on TV, quarreling in the wake of the murder. You often see it in the way the much-heralded national team plays soccer.

Proud of their superior skills, their multicultural makeup, the almost mocking manner of their free-flowing play, maddening the players of more prosaic teams, like Germany, the stars of Dutch soccer usually start their games with all the swagger of swinging Amsterdam. In their playful individualism, their progressive daringness, they know they are the best. And sometimes they are. But when things go against them and the plodding Germans, or the bloody-minded Italians, or the cussed English, go up a goal or two, the heads slump, the bickering starts, and the game is lost in a sour mood of *verongelijktheid:* Why did this have to happen to us? What did we do to deserve this? Aren't we the best? Well, fuck you!

In November 2004 things had clearly gone badly in the experimental garden. The mood of peevish disillusion was articulated most clearly by the writer Max Pam, a prominent Friend of Theo, in a television program broadcast on the day after the murder.

Pam was asked whether he really wished to leave Amsterdam and move to Germany, as had been reported. Well, said Pam, that was an exaggeration. But, as it happens, he had recently bumped into Harry Mulisch, one of Holland's most famous novelists, and Mulisch had said he no longer liked living in Holland either and was considering a move to Germany. Pam sympathized. For he, too, was fed up. What distressed him more than anything was the end of a particular way of life, a kind of "free-spirited anarchism," full of "humor and cabaret," a life where it was possible to make fun of things, to offend people without the fear of violence. "A kind of idyll," he sighed, had come to an end. Watching Pam, I kept thinking of the Dutch soccer team. After Theo's death, things were no fun anymore.

Like Heine's words, Pam's sentiments contained an element of truth. The Netherlands never was a utopia, but the world had indeed changed since 9/11, and that world had caught up with Amsterdam, just as it had with New York, Bali, Madrid, and London. The Moluccan problem was a local tragedy. But Mohammed Bouyeri, a sad loner from an Amsterdam suburb, whose social horizons had progressively narrowed to a small radicalized circle, was part of a violent wider world connected by Internet, CD-ROMs, and MSN.

4.

Amsterdam: On Sunday evening more than a thousand demonstrators remembered the Reichskristallnacht of 1938. They also reflected on recent statements of anti-Semitism. The European Commissioner, Frits Bolkestein, called the comparison of Israel to Nazi Germany "grotesque and slanderous." This is a new form of anti-Semitism which he believes is mostly confined in Western Europe to "ill-informed North African youths." VOLKSKRANT, NOVEMBER 10, 2003

Violence against Muslims in the Netherlands has strongly decreased. Acts of violence from extreme right-wing groups have also diminished. Remarkably, very few anti-Semitic incidents have been caused by people of foreign origin. This has been re-

vealed by research undertaken by the University of Leiden and
the Anne Frank Foundation in 2002.

NRC HANDELSBLAD, JANUARY 12, 2004

Holland, and Amsterdam in particular, has a long history of taking in foreigners. Sephardic Jews arrived from Antwerp and farther south in the late sixteenth and early seventeenth centuries, many of them refugees from the Spanish Inquisition. The Dutch Republic in its Golden Age was wealthy and offered religious freedom. This actually prompted many Jews, who had let their traditions lapse or been forced to convert to Catholicism, to revive their faith. A large Portuguese synagogue was built in Amsterdam between 1671 and 1675, and another was built by Polish and German Ashkenazim in 1670. For a long time, Jews, many of them very poor, suffered from all kinds of professional and social restrictions, but they were not persecuted, until the Germans arrived in 1940. This earned Amsterdam the Yiddish name of Mokum, *the* City.

The Huguenots, like the Jews, found refuge in the north from persecution. They escaped to the Dutch Republic after Louis XIV revoked their religious freedom in 1685. Holland enjoyed the fruits of the Enlightenment before most other countries in Europe. It is surely no coincidence that the so-called early Enlightenment of the Dutch Republic was partly inspired by the ideas of a son of Sephardic refugees in Amsterdam, Benedictus (Baruch) de Spinoza.

Holland's reputation for hospitality is deserved, but immigration in the twentieth century is also a story of horror, opportunism, postcolonial obligations, and an odd combination of charity and indifference. Few Jewish refugees from Nazi Germany—Anne Frank was, for example, one who did not—survived the German occupation. Their fate was certainly not welcomed by most gentiles in Holland, but despite the bravery of many individuals, too little was done to help them. Altogether 71 percent of all Jews in the Netherlands ended up in death camps, the highest percentage in Europe outside Poland. That is the horror that still hangs over Dutch life like a toxic cloud. Largely unmentioned until the 1960s, the shame of it poisons national debates to this day.

The end of empire in the Dutch East Indies, despite the problems with Moluccans, was less traumatic. The violence happened too far away. And those Eurasians and Indonesians who chose to move to the Netherlands in the 1940s and 1950s were relatively small in number, generally well educated, and easily absorbed. The same was true of the first wave of Surinamese from the former colony of Dutch Guiana. Arriving in the 1960s, when the Dutch economy boomed, these mostly middle-class men and women found work as nurses, civil servants, or teachers. The dirty work, in the boom years, was done by "guest workers" from Turkey and Morocco, single men cooped up in cheap hostels, prepared to do almost anything to provide for their families back home. These men were not expected to stay. One of them was Mohammed Bouyeri's father.

It was the second wave of Surinamese, arriving around 1972, that began to cause problems. Newly independent Suriname was shedding people, hundreds of thousands of them, mostly the descendants of African slaves. It is said that a sign at Paramaribo airport read: "Will the last Surinamese please turn off the lights." The oil shock in 1973, when Arab oil producers punished the Netherlands with an embargo for its support of Israel in the Yom Kippur War, had created a crisis in the Dutch economy. There were no longer enough jobs for the guest workers from Turkey or Morocco, let alone more than two hundred thousand newcomers from a Caribbean backwater.

The result was widespread unemployment, dependence on the welfare state, petty crime, and a vicious circle of social discrimination and sporadic violence. There are still many Surinamese without an official job, perhaps as many as 30 percent, but the Surinamese are no longer a "problem." They always speak Dutch, excel at soccer, and by and large have been moving steadily into the middle class. Like the West Indians in Britain, they are not universally welcomed, but are still recognized as an exotic yet integral part of the national culture.

The same is not true of the guest workers and their offspring. Like the Moluccans, these men were not regarded as immigrants. Their stay was supposed to have been temporary, to clean out oil tankers, work in steel factories, sweep the streets. When many of them elected to remain, the government took the benevolent view that in that case they should be joined by their wives and children. Slowly, almost without anyone's noticing, old working-class Dutch neighborhoods lost their white populations and were transformed into "dish cities" linked to Morocco, Turkey, and the Middle East by satellite television and the Internet. Gray Dutch streets filled up, not only with satellite dishes, but with Moroccan bakeries, Turkish kebab joints, travel agents offering cheap flights to Istanbul or Casablanca, and coffeehouses filled with sad-eyed men in djellabas whose health had often been wrecked by years of dirty and dangerous labor. Their wives, isolated in cramped modern apartment blocks, usually failed to learn Dutch, had little knowledge of the strange land in which they had been dumped, sometimes to be married to strange men, and had to be helped in the simplest tasks by their children, who learned faster how to cope without necessarily feeling at home.

The Turks, backed by a variety of social and religious institutions, formed a relatively close-knit community of shop-keepers and professionals. Grocery stores in Amsterdam are often owned by Turks, and so are pizzerias. If Turks turn to crime, it is organized crime, sometimes linked to the old country—financial fraud, illegal immigration, hard drugs. There are links to political violence in Turkey, to do with militant nationalism or the Kurdish question, but not so much with revolutionary Islam. That appears to be more a Moroccan problem.

Moroccans in the Netherlands are mostly Berbers, not Arabs, from remote villages in the Rif mountains. Like Sicilian peasants, they are clannish people, widely distrusted by urban Moroccans, and often, especially the women, illiterate. Less organized, with the narrow horizons of village folk, and awkwardly wedged between the North African and European worlds, Moroccan immigrants lack the kinds of institutional support that give the Turkish immigrants a sense of belonging.

Those who manage, through intelligence, perseverance, and good fortune, to make their way in Dutch society, often do very well indeed. Those who don't, for one reason or another, drift easily into a seedy world without exit of gang violence and petty crime. Most vulnerable of all are those who find their ambitions blocked despite their attempts to fit in with the mainstream of Dutch life. Anything can trigger a mood of violent resentment and self-destruction: a job offer withdrawn, a grant not given, one too many doors shut in one's face. Such a man was Mohammed Bouyeri, who adopted a brand of Islamic extremism unknown to his father, a broken-backed former guest worker from the Rif mountains, and decided to join a war against the society from which he felt excluded. Unsure of where he belonged, he lost himself in a murderous cause.

During the last few decades, the guest workers and their children were joined by another group of newcomers, many of them scarred by political violence: Tamils from Sri Lanka, Syrians and Iranians, Somali escapees from civil war, Iraqis, Bosnians, Egyptians, Chinese, and many more. Since Holland, like all European countries, almost never accepts immigrants who come for economic reasons, people try to get in as asylum seekers. Some are in genuine danger, some are not, but until recently, most managed, in one way or another, to stay on, legally or otherwise. When an Israeli cargo plane crashed into a poor suburb of Amsterdam in 1992, the number of victims was impossible to calculate, since the housing estates were filled with illegals. Even the official statistics in Amsterdam are remarkable. In 1999, 45 percent of the population was of foreign origin. If projections are right, this will be 52 percent in 2015. And the majority will be Muslim.

5.

Afshin Ellian, rightly, made a name for himself as an expert critic of the Iranian regime, which he knew from the inside. Then something went wrong. He took the role upon himself of the ultra-right-wing critic of the soft multi-culti left: the foreign lapdog of the right. And when he can't find the soft left, he will make it up. In doing so, he adopts a tone that does not exist among Dutch writers. RONALD PLASTERK IN *VOLKSKRANT,* JULY 15, 2005

Does a civilized society need religion? Historian Jonathan Israel wrote Radical Enlightenment *about the philosophical current which had no room for God. He says: "Hirsi Ali is an heir to Spinoza."* YORAM STEIN IN *TROUW,* MAY 6, 2005

I first saw Afshin Ellian at his home, a modern two-story family house in a suburb between Amsterdam and Utrecht. The only sign of anything untoward was the patrol car that passed by every so often to keep an eye on things. Our second meeting was at Leiden University, where he teaches law. A bodyguard guided me to his office and watched while we had lunch in the canteen. I noticed many female students wearing Muslim headscarves. The last time I saw Ellian, a team of bodyguards carefully checked out the café where we met and kept our table under close surveillance.

And all this because this thirty-nine-year-old scholar, born in Tehran, acquired the "dangerous hobby" of writing a newspaper column that is harshly critical of political Islam. Like Ayaan Hirsi Ali, he is seen by some as a dangerous agitator, and by others as a hero who arrived from the Muslim world to shake the Dutch from their deep sleep. This is what he believes: Citizenship of a democratic state means living by the laws of the country. A liberal democracy cannot survive when part of the population believes that divine laws trump those made by man. The fruits of the European Enlightenment must be defended, with force if necessary. It is time for Muslims to be enlightened too. European intellectuals, in their self-hating nihilism and utopian anti-Americanism, have lost the stomach to fight for Enlightenment values. The multicultural dream is over. The West, except for the U.S., is too afraid to use its power. The European welfare state is a disastrous, patronizing system that treats people like patients. The Dutch government must act to protect those who criticize Islam. No religion or minority should be immune to censure or ridicule. The solution to the Muslim problem is a Muslim Voltaire, a Muslim Nietzsche—that is to say, people like "us, the heretics—me, Salman Rushdie, Ayaan Hirsi Ali."

The tone of his columns is sometimes strident, even shrill. In person, Ellian is more humorous, but his wit is barbed, and can be sarcastic in the somewhat heavy manner of a Marxist pamphleteer. Ellian was once a man of the far left, a member of the Tudeh Party in Iran. Even he, a political refugee, who arrived in the Netherlands only in 1989, cannot resist an allusion to World War II. Observing the way Dutch authorities have dealt with the Islamist danger, he told me, made him understand why so many Dutch people had collaborated with the Nazis. He thinks the Dutch are hopelessly weak.

Under the roly-poly demeanor and the dry chuckle runs a hard current of anger. In a television program broadcast hours after the murder of Van Gogh, Ellian couldn't contain himself when a Moroccan-Dutch writer expressed the view that Bouyeri's deed could not be explained by Islam alone, and pointed to the general "polarization" of Dutch society. Jabbing his finger at the man like an interrogator, Ellian shouted that Bouyeri had gone to the mosque, had an imam, had read the Koran—"He murdered in the name of a perverted prophet!"

Afshin Ellian is angry first of all at the Islamist revolutionaries, whose brutality he witnessed as a teenager in Ayatollah Khomeini's Tehran. Like Ayaan Hirsi Ali, who experienced religious fundamentalism in Saudi Arabia and then joined the Muslim Brotherhood in Kenya, Ellian saw the violence of political Islam firsthand. This has shaped—some might say warped—his view of Islamism ever since. When

Ellian sees Mohammed B., he sees a history of torture, prisons, executions, and mass slaughter in holy wars.

Of course, a suburb of Amsterdam, however receptive some of its inhabitants may be to the call of murder and martyrdom, is not Tehran. Things are different in the flat, prosperous land of green polders and dykes, where conflicts are solved through compromise and negotiation. Ellian might be seen as an excitable foreigner, flying off the handle "in a tone that does not exist among Dutch writers." Then again, that is what people resting in the comfort of liberal democracies said about refugees from the Third Reich and dissidents under Communism. Amsterdam *is* different from Tehran, to be sure, but Ellian is neither a politician nor a diplomat, but a lifelong dissident, for whom compromise spells weakness.

What enraged Ellian was not just the inability of other non-Western immigrants to understand and abide by the laws that guaranteed their liberty but, worse in his eyes, the inability of Europeans to appreciate what they had. Ellian, and others like him, including Ayaan Hirsi Ali, are sometimes called "Enlightenment fundamentalists." This might sound like a contradiction. Thinkers of the Enlightenment, after all, rejected all dogmas. But Ellian's penchant for denunciation in the name of freedom and democracy is marked by earlier, more brutal experiences.

When things get rough, Ellian said, after I had asked him

how he put up with living dangerously, he reaches for books by Friedrich Nietzsche. Why should Westerners be the only ones to dissent from their traditions, he wondered. "Why not us? It is racist to think that Muslims are too backward to think for themselves." He spoke with passion, and more than a hint of fury. I admired his passion, but there was something unnerving about his fury, something that reminded me of Huizinga's idea that dangerous illusions come from a sense of inferiority, of a historical wrong. Ellian likes to wonder aloud, throwing up his hands in despair: Why did the great civilizations of Persia and Araby not produce a Nietzsche or a Voltaire? Why not now?

The battle is both centuries old and relatively new. Until recently not much attention was paid outside the universities to the currents and crosscurrents of the Enlightenment and the Counter-Enlightenment. It was the attack on the World Trade Center on September 11, 2001, an act of mass murder that was random as well as precisely targeted, that brought the Enlightenment back to the center of political debate, especially in Holland, one of the countries where it all began more than three hundred years ago.

Not just academics but politicians and popular columnists saw the Enlightenment as the fortress to be defended against Islamist extremism. The jihad in which Mohammed Bouyeri served as a mere footsoldier was seen, not just by Ellian and Hirsi Ali, as our contemporary Counter-

Enlightenment, and conservative politicians, such as the former VVD leader and European commissioner Frits Bolkestein, jumped into the breach for the freethinking values of Spinoza and Voltaire. One of the main claims of Enlightenment philosophy is that its ideas based on reason are by definition universal. But the Enlightenment has a particular appeal to some conservatives because its values are not just universal, but more importantly, "ours," that is, European, Western values.

Bolkestein, a former business executive with intellectual interests that set him apart from most professional politicians, was the first mainstream politician to warn about the dire consequences of accepting too many Muslim immigrants, whose customs clashed with "our fundamental values." Certain values, he claimed, such as gender equality, or the separation of church and state, are not negotiable. We met on several occasions in Amsterdam, and when it was time to part he would invariably say: "We must talk more next time about the lack of confidence in Western civilization." Like Afshin Ellian, he frets about European weakness. That is why he worries about the possibility of Turkey, with its 68 million Muslims, joining the European Union. For it would, in his view, spell the end of Europe, not as a geographical entity, but as a community of values born of the Enlightenment.

Fifteen years ago, when Bolkestein first talked about the threat to fundamental values, he was a hateful figure to the

Left, a fearmonger, even a racist. The main focus of his attack was the idea of cultural relativism, the common notion among leftists that immigrants should be allowed to retain their own "identity." But something interesting happened along the way. There is a long and frequently poisonous history in European politics of left-wing internationalism and conservative defense of traditional values. The Left was on the side of universalism, scientific socialism, and the like, while the Right believed in culture, in the sense of "our culture," "our traditions." During the multicultural age of the 1970s and 1980s, this debate began to shift. It was now the Left that stood for culture and tradition, especially "their" cultures and traditions, that is, those of the immigrants, while the Right argued for the universal values of the Enlightenment. The problem in this debate was the fuzzy border between what was in fact universal and what was merely "ours."

But the real shift came when a well-known sequence of events drove many former leftists into the conservative camp. First came the Salman Rushdie affair: "their" values were indeed clashing with "ours"; a free-spirited cosmopolitan writer was being threatened by an extreme version of an alien religion. Then New York was attacked. And now Theo van Gogh, "our" Salman Rushdie, was dead. Leftists, embittered by what they saw as the failure of multiculturalism, or fired up by the anticlericalism of their revolutionary past, joined conservatives in the battle for the Enlightenment. Bolkestein became a hero for people who used to despise him.

At first sight, the clash of values appears to be straightforward: on the one hand, secularism, science, equality between men and women, individualism, freedom to criticize without fear of violent retribution, and on the other, divine laws, revealed truth, male domination, tribal honor, and so on. It is indeed hard to see how in a liberal democracy these contrasting values can be reconciled. How could one not be on the side of Frits Bolkestein, or Afshin Ellian, or Ayaan Hirsi Ali? But a closer look reveals fissures that are less straightforward. People come to the struggle for Enlightenment values from very different angles, and even when they find common ground, their aims may be less than enlightened.

Hirsi Ali and Ellian are often accused of fighting the battles of their own past on European soil, as though they had smuggled a non-Western crisis into a peaceful Western country. Traumatized by Khomeini's revolution or an oppressive Muslim upbringing in Somalia, Saudi Arabia, and Kenya, they turned against the faith of their fathers and embraced a radical version of the European Enlightenment: Hirsi Ali as the heiress of Spinoza, and Ellian as Nietzsche's disciple. They are warriors on a battlefield inside the world of Islam. But they are also struggling against oppressive cultures that force genital mutilation on young girls and marriage with strangers on young women. The bracing air of universalism is a release from tribal traditions.

But the same could be said, in a way, of their greatest enemy: the modern holy warrior, like the killer of Theo van Gogh. The young Moroccan-Dutch youth downloading English translations of Arabic texts from the Internet is also looking for a universal cause, severed from cultural and tribal specificities. The promised purity of modern Islamism, which is after all a revolutionary creed, has been disconnected from cultural tradition. That is why it appeals to those who feel displaced, in the suburbs of Paris no less than in Amsterdam. They are stuck between cultures they find equally alienating. The war between Ellian's Enlightenment and Bouyeri's jihad is not a straightforward clash between culture and universalism, but between two different visions of the universal, one radically secular, the other radically religious. The radically secular society of post-1960s Amsterdam, which looks like the promised land to a sophisticated refugee from religious revolution, is unsettling to the confused son of an immigrant from the remote countryside of Morocco.

But not every pious Muslim is a potential terrorist. To see religion, even religious orthodoxy, as the main enemy of Enlightenment values is misleading. For even though the modern terrorist has latched onto a religious faith, he might as well have chosen—and in different times did choose—a radically secular creed to justify his thirst for violent death. Besides, there is a difference between the anticlericalism of Voltaire, who was up against one of the two most powerful institutions of eighteenth-century France, and radical secularists today battling a minority within an already embattled minority.

There is also a difference between the eighteenth-century *philosophes* and conservative Dutch politicians of the twenty-first century. The pioneers of the Enlightenment were iconoclasts, with radical ideas about politics and life. The Marquis de Sade was a typical man of the Enlightenment, as much as Diderot. In terms of Islam, Ellian and Hirsi Ali are certainly iconoclasts. It is harder to see a link between a respectable conservative EU commissioner and the great chronicler of sadism. But then, of course, a desire to smash sacred icons is not why many conservatives joined the battle for the modern Enlightenment in the first place.

The sacred icons of Dutch society were broken in the 1960s, as elsewhere in the Western world, when the churches lost their grip on people's lives, when government authority was something to challenge, not obey, when sexual taboos were publicly and privately breached, and when—rather in line with the original Enlightenment—people opened their eyes and ears to civilizations outside the West. The rebellions of the 1960s contained irrational, indeed antirational, and sometimes violent strains, and the fashion for such far-flung exotica as Maoism sometimes turned into a revolt against liberalism and democracy. One by one the religious and political pillars that supported the established order of the Netherlands were cut away. The tolerance of other cultures, often barely understood, that spread with new waves of immigration, was sometimes just that—tolerance—and sometimes sheer indifference, bred by a lack of confidence in values and institutions that needed to be defended.

The conservative call for Enlightenment values is partly a revolt against a revolt. Tolerance has gone too far for many conservatives. They believe, like some former leftists, that multiculturalism was a mistake; our fundamental values must be reclaimed. Because secularism has gone too far to bring back the authority of the churches, conservatives and neo-conservatives have latched onto the Enlightenment as a badge of national or cultural identity. The Enlightenment, in other words, has become the name for a new conservative order, and its enemies are the aliens, whose values we can't share.

Perhaps it was a necessary correction. Islamist revolution, like any violent creed, needs to be resisted, and a nation-state, to be viable, must stand for something. Political institutions are not purely mechanical. But an essential part of Enlightenment thinking is that everything, especially claims to "nonnegotiable" or "fundamental" values, should be open to criticism. The whole point of liberal democracy, its greatest strength, especially in the Netherlands, is that conflicting faiths, interests, and views can be resolved only through negotiation. The only thing that cannot be negotiated is the use of violence.

The murder of Theo van Gogh was committed by one Dutch convert to a revolutionary war, who was probably helped by others. Such revolutionaries in Europe are still few in number. But the murder, like the bomb attacks in Madrid and London, the fatwa against Salman Rushdie, and the worldwide Muslim protests against cartoons of the Prophet in a Danish newspaper, exposed dangerous fractures that run through all European nations. Islam may soon become the majority religion in countries whose churches have been turned more and more into tourist sites, apartment houses, theaters, and places of entertainment. The French scholar Olivier Roy is right: Islam is now a European religion. How Europeans, Muslims as well as non-Muslims, cope with this is the question that will decide our future. And what better place to watch the drama unfold than the Netherlands, where freedom came from a revolt against Catholic Spain, where ideals of tolerance and diversity became a badge of national honor, and where political Islam struck its first blow against a man whose deepest conviction was that freedom of speech included the freedom to insult.

TWO

Thank You, Pim

Yesterday evening I read on the front page of the NRC *Handelsblad that Ayaan Hirsi Ali was going into hiding. Fortunately my name wasn't mentioned. I'm still living at home, thank you very much, and hope to keep it that way.*

THEO VAN GOGH, SPEAKING ON LOCATION
WHILE MAKING HIS LAST FILM, *06/05*

1.

On the morning that Theo van Gogh was shot, he was cycling toward his office in the south of Amsterdam to do some postproduction work on *06/05*, a Hitchcockian thriller about the assassination of Pim Fortuyn, the populist outsider who almost became prime minister. The movie was a departure for Van Gogh. Thrillers hadn't been his thing. But he had long been obsessed with Fortuyn, whose murder on May 6, 2002, provoked an extraordinary outburst of shock, grief, anger, and quasi-religious hysteria. The man who would soon become prime minister, Jan Peter Balkenende, not a man blessed with great imagination, reached for appropriate words to describe the situation. All he could come up with was "un-Dutch."

Van Gogh's movie spins an elaborate conspiracy theory involving the secret service, led by a fat gay man wearing lipstick, American arms dealers, far right politicians, and a sexy animal rights activist of Turkish descent. Van Gogh never saw the film in its final version. The conspiracy is implausible, to say the least. But the picture of Dutch society, in all its post-multi-culti confusion, is convincing. It may look "un-Dutch" to a small-town Calvinist prime minister, but it shows what life is like in the urban triangle of Amsterdam, The Hague, and Rotterdam, an area of mass immigration, American pop fashions, and green fields disappearing rapidly under more and more layers of concrete. What Van Gogh got was the air of menace simmering under the placid surface, menace that could suddenly erupt in an act of senseless violence.

It was the most sensational political murder in the Netherlands since 1672, when the brothers Jan and Cornelis de Witt were literally ripped to pieces by a lynch mob in The Hague. During its Golden Age, the seventeenth-century Dutch Republic was split by a power struggle between a paternalistic republican merchant elite, known as *regenten,* and the monarchists, led by the House of Orange and backed by the interfering Calvinist Church. The mob, especially at a time of economic crisis, was on the side of monarchy and church. The *regenten* were regarded as haughty, self-interested, and dangerously liberal. The De Witt brothers, friends of Spinoza, were typical *regenten*.

Pim Fortuyn, whose rise in Dutch politics had been as sudden as it was steep, was no De Witt. On the contrary, though he was neither a Calvinist nor an ardent monarchist, his agitation was largely directed at what he described, sarcastically, as "Our Kind of People," the contemporary *regenten*, members of a powerful "left-wing Church," who looked after their own interests while ignoring the concerns of the common people. Fortuyn's program could be summed up in negatives; he was against bureaucracy, leftist *regenten*, and immigration, especially Muslim immigration. He was also proudly, even flamboyantly, homosexual.

Theo van Gogh fell under the shaven-headed dandy's spell, and often gave Fortuyn informal advice, phoning "the divine baldy" when he was excited about something, which was most of the time. When Fortuyn appeared as a guest on Van Gogh's chat show, Theo jokingly suggested that they run for office on the same ticket. One of his ideas was for Fortuyn to campaign in the company of a Muslim woman dressed in a burqa. Fortuyn declined, but some of his best lines were in fact written by Van Gogh. In their outrageousness they understood one another, were kindred spirits, even. And they would be inextricably linked in death.

It is hard to say which had the greater impact on society,

but the two murders are connected in ways that are not always obvious. To almost universal relief, Fortuyn was not killed by a Muslim jihadi of foreign descent, but by an earnest Dutch animal rights activist on a bicycle, named Volkert van der Graaf. (The fact that both killers arrived on bikes added a peculiarly Dutch flavor to their murders.) It happened a few minutes after 6:00 P.M., at the Media Park of Hilversum, where Fortuyn had just concluded a long radio interview. Tired from campaigning, but in a buoyant mood, Fortuyn, carrying a bottle of champagne, was just about to slide into his dark blue Daimler, where Kenneth and Carla, his two cocker spaniels, were patiently waiting, when Van der Graaf, a small man in a baseball cap, shot him five times in the head and neck with a semiautomatic pistol. Van der Graaf had never been to the Media Park before. He had downloaded maps, as well as Fortuyn's schedule, from the Internet.

Exactly what prompted Van der Graaf's action was never clear. Van Gogh's film is not really concerned with Van der Graaf's motives. All we know is that Van der Graaf was a sworn enemy of factory farming, and mink farmers in particular, whom he pursued through the law courts with considerable success. Fortuyn liked to sport fur collars on his winter coats, and did once write that "we must stop all this whining about nature and the environment." As far as he was concerned, fur farms should be allowed to continue. But Van der Graaf appears to have been bothered by other aspects of Fortuyn, to do more with personality than any specific environmental policies. His hatred was moral more than political.

He thought Fortuyn was like Hitler, but not because he was a mass murderer. In some ways, Van der Graaf's idea of Hitler sounded more like the seventeenth-century mob's image of the De Witt brothers. What he objected to was Fortuyn's "opportunism," his "unwillingness to sacrifice his own interests," his "arrogance" toward the weak and vulnerable. Above all, he objected to his "vanity," his ostentatiousness, his "pride." Just the look of him was objectionable: the flashy suits, the loud Windsor-knotted ties, the silk handkerchiefs spilling rather too copiously from the pin-striped breast pocket. Fortuyn was a showboat. And that, in a nation where "if you behave normally, you are already behaving madly enough," is a grave accusation. Van der Graaf took this puritanical Dutch homily to a murderous extreme. He may have been a pathetic figure, but he was, in his way, a man of principle, to the point of being a fanatic. It is a characteristic of Calvinism to hold moral principles too rigidly, and this might be considered a vice as well as a virtue of the Dutch. It played a part in the makeup of Van der Graaf, as well as Mohammed Bouyeri, and even Theo van Gogh. The two killings, of Van Gogh and Fortuyn, were principled murders.

Volkert van der Graaf was always a difficult child. He was born in 1969, in the same small-town Protestant environment as Prime Minister Balkenende. His mother was a strict evangelical Christian, born in England, his father a biology teacher. Nature, animals, were always the center of Volkert's world. When he was fifteen, he found work in a shelter for injured birds, but was soon dismissed for being impossible, arguing about everything, removing mousetraps to save the mice that harmed the birds, and so on. He hated the fact that his parents ate meat, refused to sit on his parents' leather sofa, and never dined at home. While failing to complete his studies in "environmental hygiene" at the university of agriculture in Wageningen, he became a fervent antivivisectionist and a dogged enemy of intensive farming. Apart from the occasional flash of temper, Volkert was known as a taciturn, inconspicuous fellow, a bore more than a potential murderer. In 2001 he fell in love with an older woman. They had a baby daughter, and though a proud father, he appeared to be under pressure. Perhaps he was depressed. In any case, Volkert felt he had to do something big to protect the weak and vulnerable.

2.

Fortuyn's funeral was an extraordinary spectacle, something fit for a beloved queen or a pope. He would have adored it. As a boy, Fortuyn had fantasies of being the pope.

His brother and sister were made to kneel before him as worshipful priests. These daydreams lasted well into his puberty. "Where other Catholic boys might have wanted to become bishops," he told a reporter, "only the highest was good enough for me. It shows my extravagance, I suppose." Pages of his autobiography are devoted to a description of Pope Pius XII's funeral. He was also impressed by the ceremony around the death of Maria Callas. All very un-Dutch.

The funeral cortège slowly made its way through the crowds in Rotterdam, tens of thousands cheering and throwing flowers in its way. The long white funeral car was followed by Fortuyn's own Daimler, driven by his butler, Herman, who listened impassively as the Slave Chorus from *Nabucco* was blasted through the car speakers. On the front seat, next to the butler, sat Kenneth and Carla, the pet spaniels. Along with the coffin, the dogs were led into the Laurentius and Elizabeth Cathedral for the funeral mass. Crowds gazed adoringly on the scene, rolling their eyes and screaming "Pimmy, thank you, Pimmy, thank you!" Some began to sing the English soccer anthem, "You'll Never Walk Alone." They also sang the supporters' anthems to the local soccer team, Feyenoord.

Soccer anthems might seem out of place at the funeral of a politician who never showed the slightest interest in sports. *Nabucco* was much more his thing. But on reflection, they are not so strange after all. The stadium has largely replaced the church as a place for community singing and other expressions of collective devotion. And the emotions stirred up by Fortuyn—tribal nostalgia, distrust of outsiders, hero worship—were precisely those of soccer fans.

When the coffin arrived, the crowds went wild, keening and whistling and hollering as though the home team had scored a goal. Every guest inside the cathedral was presented with a white rose. Ad Melkert, the Social Democrat leader, a studious, balding figure in glasses, was spotted by one of Fortuyn's followers, a well-dressed middle-aged lady, who hissed: "Now you've got what you wanted, you bastard!" It was an extraordinary moment: a typical earnest politician of the center-left, who had always assumed he was on the side of "the people," had become a hate figure, who might, in different times and different circumstances, have been lynched by the mob. An usher handed the woman a white rose. Kenneth and Carla began to bark.

"God has a mission for you," said a postcard signed by forty men in Zeeland, the native province of Volkert van der Graaf and Jan Peter Balkenende. Another admirer saw Fortuyn as "a white-winged angel." A young woman, visiting a small museum in Rotterdam containing Fortuyn memorabilia, believed that "such a man is born only once in a thousand years." Letters arrived after the funeral with images of the Virgin Mary, the Italian holy man Padre Pio, and Pim Fortuyn. Clemens van Herwaarden, a researcher in Amsterdam, wrote his thesis on Fortuyn as the Messiah. He said: "People who feel unrepresented by any political party, who are relatively ignorant, and who get most of their information from television, such people saw Fortuyn as more than a political leader; he was a savior."[1]

In November 2004, a few weeks after Van Gogh's murder, a television poll was held to determine the greatest figure in Dutch history—inspired by a similar BBC poll on the greatest Englishman (Winston Churchill). Pim Fortuyn came out on top, above William the Silent, Rembrandt, and Erasmus. Spinoza didn't even make the list. Anne Frank might well have, but since she did not carry a Dutch passport when she was murdered, she could not be included. (A question was raised in parliament as to the possibility of granting her Dutch citizenship posthumously. The idea was rejected, however, since it was deemed to be unfair to other victims of the Holocaust.) In any event, a statue of Pim Fortuyn was erected by the city of Rotterdam in the middle of the business district. His bald bronze head shines brightly over a black granite plinth, the mouth wide open, as though he is about to give a speech. The words *Loquendi libertatem custodiamus* (Let us protect the freedom of speech) are engraved in the stone. Every day people come to lay fresh flowers at his feet.

Savior, angel, the greatest Dutchman in history—all this for a politician whose career began only in 1999, when he was chosen as a candidate for a new party started by a louche assortment of real estate developers, advertising men, and an ex–disk jockey. When he died, Fortuyn hadn't even made it into the national parliament, let alone the cabinet. A Roman Catholic fantasizer, a gay man who talked openly of sexual adventures in bathhouses and "backrooms," a show-off with the gaudy style of a showbiz impresario. How was it possible for such a man to become so popular in a country known for its Calvinist restraint, its bourgeois disdain for excesses, its phlegmatic preference for consensus and compromise?

3.

Fortuyn hated being compared to notorious figures of the European far right such as France's Jean-Marie Le Pen or Austria's Jörg Haider. He didn't even regard himself as particularly right-wing. When the BBC reporter John Simpson suggested that Fortuyn's desire to close the Dutch borders to foreign immigrants might be construed as racist, Fortuyn lost his cool, insulting Simpson in broken English and terminating the interview. He was thin-skinned in that way.

It is true that Fortuyn was no Haider or Le Pen; he was something more interesting: a populist who played on the fear of Muslims while boasting of having sex with Moroccan boys; a reactionary who denounced Islam for being a danger to Dutch liberties; a social climber who saw himself as an outsider battling the elite. Still, if Fortuyn was not simply a far-right demagogue, like Haider or Le Pen, he did tap into some of the same anxieties that swept across many parts of Europe and beyond. To a confused people, afraid of being swamped by immigrants and worried that pan-European or global institutions were rapidly taking over their lives, Fortuyn promised a way back to simpler times, when, to paraphrase the late Queen Wilhelmina, we were still ourselves, when everyone was white, and upstanding Dutchmen were in control of the nation's destiny. He was a peddler of nostalgia.

My grandmother once remarked that life would be so much simpler if Holland were to have just three political parties: Protestant, Catholic, and Socialist. She said this in the 1930s, when many Protestants refused to patronize Catholic stores and vice versa, and marriages outside of the faith were almost unheard of. She said it when many Europeans were calling for strong men to stop the rot, and Johan Huizinga wrote his famous essay to discourage such sentiments. My grandmother had no fascist sympathies. But she was too simplistic. After all, the Protestant church had many denominations, and they all wanted their own representation. Laissez-faire liberals, too, had their own distinctly non-socialist party.

Religious and political affiliations were not just a question of parties. Every aspect of social life, what we now call civil society—sports clubs, schools, broadcasting stations, trade unions—was organized along these lines. They were called "pillars." From the cabinet minister down to the lowest manual worker, everyone was part of one of the pillars that held up the edifice of Dutch society, and all the real or potential conflicts between the pillars were negotiated by the gentlemen who stood at their pinnacles. This is how centuries of religious strife ended in an admirable spirit of compromise, as soggy as the Dutch landscape reclaimed from a sometimes turbulent sea.

Times changed, of course, and old rivalries dissolved to make room for new ones. As church attendance dropped, drastically after the 1960s, the remaining Catholics and Protestants found a common home in one Christian Democratic Party. When the socialism in social democracy faded with the fall of Communism in the 1980s, this too paved the way for new alliances, based more on convenience than political ideas.

Since ideology and class conflict were no longer a basis for party politics, something else had to take their place. In the 1990s the "red" Social Democrats mixed with the "blue" free-market conservatives to come up with "purple" coalitions. Politicians proudly hailed the new politics as the "polder model," a system based on the same spirit of negotiation and watery compromise that informed the politics of the pillars. Up to a point, it worked. The Netherlands was prosperous and exuded an outward calm. People were, it appeared, *satisfait*.

The polder model suited the Dutch. The great and the good who had once ruled the pillars, and now the welfare state, were in many respects just like the *regenten* of the seventeenth century. You see their countenances perfectly portrayed in the Golden Age paintings of Frans Hals: seated around their oak tables in solid, barely decorated rooms, dressed in sober black, administering poorhouses and orphanages, dispensing charity to the needy, discussing the affairs of business and state, these well-meaning, prosperous, but never, *ever* ostentatious notables, these excellent gentlemen of substance, have a look of probity, thrift, hard work, tolerance, and—this is the genius of Frans Hals—the ineffable smugness of superior virtue. Here was Dutch republicanism at the height of its glory: a virtuous elite of Our Kind of People discreetly wielding power, supposedly for the common good, and brooking no interference.

I have seen these faces, time and again, in the VIP boxes of sports stadiums, at parliamentary debates, at concerts and royal festivities, that same look of quiet self-satisfaction, not because of any great wealth or personal achievement, but by sheer dint of virtuously and reasonably running the affairs of a small nation where all people of consequence know one another well. (Which is not to say they like each other, of course.) These were the typical faces of "purple" too. Ladies and gentlemen in sober suits who regarded it as their God-given duty to take care of the unfortunate, the sick, the asylum seekers from abroad, and the guest workers. That is what the welfare state was for. That is how the polder model was run, from the discreetly appointed offices of the modern-day *regenten*.

By the 1990s, cracks had begun to appear in the purple veneer. For one thing, as in all European countries, the authority of national governments was slowly being eroded by European institutions and multinational corporations. Mounting problems, to do with pensions, health care, crime, taxes, appeared to be slipping from the grasp of nationally elected politicians. Years of officially promoted European idealism and denigration of national sentiment added to a growing sense of unease. What was it, in a world of multinational business and pan-European bureaucracy, to be Dutch, or French, or German? People were beginning to feel unrepresented. They no longer knew who was really in charge. This is when the modern *regenten,* like Ad Melkert, the Social Democrat, began to lose their grip on popular sentiment. Worse than irrelevant, they began to be targets of active hostility.

The politics of consensus contains its own forms of corruption: politics gets stuck in the rut of a self-perpetuating elite, shuffling jobs back and forth between members of the club. This happened in Austria, where Social and Christian Democrats had been in power for too long. It happened in India, where Congress had ruled for decades. It happened in the purple Netherlands too. Without ideology, and with nothing but jobs for the boys at stake, party politics was losing its raison d'être, and trust in the old democratic order could no longer be taken for granted.

Muslim immigration was only the most visible focus of popular unease. People in The Hague or Rotterdam were used to seeing shabby areas of relative deprivation around the main railway stations. Now these areas were looking increasingly foreign, more like Edirne or Fez. For a long time, it was not "done" to see anything problematic in these changes. Multiculturalism was the orthodoxy of the purple governments. To question this orthodoxy, or to worry about the social consequences of such swift changes in the urban landscape, was to risk being called a racist. When Fortuyn made disparaging remarks about Islam, leaders from the mainstream parties talked about "Nazism."

Once again the shadow of World War II fell over the politics of the present. Comparisons were made between "Islamophobia" and anti-Semitism. Anne Frank's name was invoked in parliament as a warning. Never again, said the well-meaning defenders of the multicultural ideal, must Holland betray a religious minority. Those hundred thousand Jews still haunted the collective memory as a shameful reminder. In political circles, it was sometimes Jewish survivors, such as Ed van Thijn, the former mayor of Amsterdam, who made this point most forcefully. They did so with good intentions, but instead of encouraging debate, such moral reminders tended to result in pained silence. Except in the case of Theo van Gogh. His response was to go for the ultimate shock effect, by indulging in the crassest, most revolting taunts against Jews. However, both Van Gogh and some of his critics were missing the point. For Jews were never the issue.

Criminality in certain immigrant areas was becoming a serious problem. Too many people were living in the larger cities illegally. Cases of theft, drug dealing, even serious street violence went unprosecuted, and usually unreported. There was a feeling in major cities that the police had lost control of the streets and criminals could do as they liked. When a number of Social Democrats tried to raise the matter inside their party, the PVDA, they were told to switch the subject. It was not even permissible for newspaper reporters to mention the ethnic background of criminals, for this would have revealed patterns that were better left unspoken. A former PVDA leader, Felix Rottenberg, believes that "feelings of guilt of the postwar generation had a huge influence on politically correct thinking." Guilt, that is, for what their parents had allowed to happen while looking the other way. People were still looking away, but from a different problem.

Some politicians, such as Frits Bolkestein, then leader of the free-market conservatives, or VVD, did raise the matter, as did a left-wing sociologist named Paul Scheffer in an explosive essay entitled "The Multicultural Drama." Bolkestein warned of clashing values. Scheffer analyzed the dangers of isolated, alienated foreign communities undermining the social cohesion of Dutch society. Both were denounced as racists. To see massive immigration as a problem at all was, in respectable circles, worse than bad taste; it was like questioning the European ideal or racial equality. The twin evils of World War II, as everyone knew, were nationalism and racism. Any hint of a revival would have to be squashed at once. This was understandable, perhaps even laudable. But it didn't stop many people from feeling that Europeanism and multiculturalism were the ideals of a complacent elite, of the modern-day *regenten*. What such people were waiting for was a politician who was crass enough to express their anxieties and break the discussion wide open. That man was Pim Fortuyn.

4.

Max Pam, the distinguished writer and Friend of Theo, did not vote for Pim Fortuyn. But like other former leftists, he is disillusioned with what he regards as the moralistic complacency of the social-democratic political class. We had dinner one night at his rambling house in the quiet and verdant streets of south Amsterdam. Not too far from where we were was one of the densest immigrant areas in the city. Mohammed Bouyeri lived there until the day he murdered Van Gogh. It was not far in geographical distance, but many miles away socially. Pam had grown up in that part of town himself, when it had just been built in the 1950s in a spurt of social-democratic idealism, a district of affordable homes for young low- and middle-income families. It is now one of Amsterdam's largest "dish cities," mostly inhabited by people of Turkish and Moroccan descent, wired to the Islamic world through satellite TV.

We had an argument about Fortuyn, and his extraordinary popularity among people with whom he could not have had anything in common. Fortuyn was often described as a *relnicht*, a "screaming queen." Discretion was certainly not his style. But openly gay men, let alone screamers, do not, as a rule, become successful right-wing populists. People searching for political messiahs tend to look elsewhere. And yet they saw Fortuyn as an angelic savior. Pam believed that this happened *despite* Fortuyn's open homosexuality. The main issue, in his view, was fear of Muslim immigrants. The Dutch, he said, were not racists. But successive Dutch governments had been far too tolerant of intolerance. They should never have allowed those dish cities to grow into hotbeds of religious bigotry. The streets in which he once played had become "like the South Bronx."

I had been to Overtoomse Veld, and the South Bronx it was surely not. The problems of immigration clearly had much to do with Fortuyn's popularity. But I think his baroque style, his being a *relnicht,* may actually have added to his special aura, the mystique of a man who came from nowhere—from heaven, perhaps—to save his fellow countrymen. In many traditional communities, in Asia, but also southern Europe, transsexuals and transvestites play important roles in sacred ceremonies. They are different, and thus discriminated against. Most make a living as prostitutes. But they also inspire a kind of mystical awe. For like angels, they are above the mundane lives of ordinary men and women.

Fortuyn himself, the man who would be pope, saw a connection between sex and religion. In April 1999 he gave a fascinating interview to *Trouw,* a newspaper that used to be the official organ of the Calvinist pillar and still has a strong interest in spiritual affairs. The interviewer asked Fortuyn to give his personal views on the Ten Commandments. In his response to "Thou Shalt Not Commit Adultery" he talked at length about having sex with many men in the darkened backrooms of gay bars in Rotterdam. One place he frequented was called Shaft; another was Mateloos, or Boundless, a word he liked to apply to himself.

"I don't mean to be blasphemous," he said, "but I have

to say that the atmosphere of Catholic liturgy comes back to me in the backrooms of gentlemen's clubs. The backroom I frequent in Rotterdam is not totally dark. Filtered light leaks into the room, just like in an ancient cathedral. There is something religious about having sex in such a place. Religiosity and coming together—sometimes achieved in sex—can be two sides of the same coin. . . . A backroom is certainly erotically exciting. More exciting than a church? Well, you won't hear me say that. I found it very thrilling to be an altar boy. Let's judge things by their own merits."[2]

Not exactly the sort of thing one would hear from Le Pen, or Haider. But then, Fortuyn was not always a man of the right. As a young academic in Groningen, he was a socialist, a loyal member of the Social Democrats—as, by the way, were the young Theo van Gogh, as well as his killer, Mohammed Bouyeri, and Ayaan Hirsi Ali, who wrote the film that gave rise to the murder. Nor was immigration always an issue for him. This began only after he moved to Rotterdam in the early 1990s, to become a sociology professor. Local immigrant youths smashed the windows of Boundless and threatened its clientele. Fortuyn suddenly felt vulnerable in a country where he had thought he was safe. This had a profound effect on his political thinking.

In February 2002, a reporter asked him why he felt so strongly about Islam. "I have no desire," he replied, "to have to go through the emancipation of women and ho-mosexuals all over again. There are many gay high school teachers who are afraid of revealing their identity because of Turkish and Moroccan boys in their classes. I find that scandalous."

Did he feel personally threatened? "No, I'm not a timid man." So why the hatred of Islam? "I don't hate Islam. I find it a backward culture. I have traveled in many parts of the world. Wherever Islam rules, it's simply ghastly. All that am-biguity. They're a bit like those old Calvinists. Calvinists are always lying. Why? Because their moral principles are raised so high that it's not humanly possible to live up to them. You see the same thing in Muslim culture. Now look at the Netherlands. Where could a candidate for a huge political movement such as my own be openly gay? I take pride in that. And I'd like to keep it that way."[3]

There was a sexual element even in his nostalgia for the stern comforts of an older, more disciplined order. Memories of his favorite primary school teacher inspired the following reverie: "He was a big man in every respect, his height, his posture, and especially those hands! A rumor had it that he laid one of the difficult boys over his knee and spanked his ass with those big hands of his. The boy couldn't sit down for a day. Apocryphal in this case, perhaps. But that kind of thing worked." Fortuyn believed that the educational reformers of the 1960s, "those newfangled theoreticians in leisure wear," brought this grim idyll to an end. A yearning for discipline would remain part of his nostalgic reveries.

Fortuyn wrote many books, about the purple governments, about the dangers of Islam, about his own life. At one time, he was a successful political columnist for a conservative journal, and a highly paid speaker, much in demand from chambers of commerce, military bases, and business groups of various kinds. But his real talent was not as a writer, let alone a thinker. His insights were mostly banal, when not simply misinformed. He was never taken seriously by the professors, whose praise and recognition he once craved. Fortuyn's genius was theatrical. Self-presentation was his greatest talent. The transformation from a mediocre academic into a popular cult figure was his final masterpiece.

You can see the transformation take place in his photographs. People remember his narcissism at Groningen University, where his office was decorated with a huge portrait of himself. But in the early pictures, Fortuyn still looks unremarkable, a balding, bearded sociologist, a figure rather like Ad Melkert. A little better dressed than most academics, perhaps, but nothing special. It was later, in the 1990s, when he shaved off all his remaining hair (for an audience at the Vatican), that the image of Pim Fortuyn, *relnicht,* savior, scourge of Our Kind of People, fell into place. Part walking penis, part phony aristocrat, Fortuyn became a presence, in

TV studios, on radio programs, and at public debates, that could not be ignored. Even the voice—a peculiar mixture of camp and menace—was mesmerizing.

One of the highlights of Fortuyn's short career was his performance in a television debate in 2002 with other party leaders. In terms of social background, they were more or less equals. None of the party leaders, not the later prime minister, Balkenende, a Christian Democrat, nor Ad Melkert, or even Hans Dijkstal, the conservative leader, had a background that could be called remotely upper-class. But the Dutch political elite is not an aristocracy. It is defined less by class than by attitude, of virtue, sobriety, and unquestioned authority. Our Kind of People, on the whole, are also extraordinarily dull.

And there was Fortuyn, flush from a huge electoral upset. His upstart party of dodgy amateurs had swamped the city council of Rotterdam. The party elders were outraged, especially Melkert, who could not even bring himself to look Fortuyn in the eye, let alone congratulate him. The more churlishly his rivals behaved, the more Fortuyn hit his stride, using his body like a trained actor: teasing, joking, mocking, cajoling—all in that high-pitched, teasing tone. An arched eyebrow, a slight flutter of the eyelashes, was enough to make the earnest *regenten* look like gauche schoolboys who failed to see the joke at their expense. One couldn't keep one's eyes off the man. Never before had Dutch politicians looked so foolish. Their carefully nurtured facade of quiet authority lay in tatters. It virtually ended Melkert's career. The *relnicht* had won.

5.

The son of a traveling salesman (in envelopes), whom he despised, and a doting mother, who indulged his fantasies of being her "crown prince," Fortuyn always felt like an outsider. That was a large part of his appeal to all those who felt excluded, in terms of class, wealth, prestige, or power. Even religion may have played a part. The Fortuyns were Catholics in a largely Protestant small town. At school, Fortuyn always wore a suit and tie, eccentric even in more formal times. He was not interested in sports, let alone girls.

"I want to belong," he wrote in his autobiography, *Babyboomers,* "but I don't belong . . . since my earliest childhood years I felt different and peculiar. . . . Whenever I forgot how different I was, my friends and their parents would remind me of it. . . . I was always special, in the way I dressed, spoke, and behaved." He knew why, or at least he thought he did: "Being an outsider is part of my character. I'm 'a man in his own right' and that has to do with my homosexuality."[4]

Wishing to belong, yet taking a special pride in being different, is not unusual among minorities. The desire to conform to an ideal that is out of reach can turn into a kind of mockery. Benjamin Disraeli saved the English aristocracy in a bourgeois age by flattering their self-image in a bizarre form of mimicry of their manners. Yet the aristocrats never quite trusted him, as though he were really playing some elaborate trick at their expense. Oscar Wilde, the Irish dandy, took his climb into the English upper class very seriously, yet never missed a chance to ridicule it. Such men know they will never quite belong. But they like to imagine that they do, in a form of theater that verges on satire.

Fortuyn bought a house in Rotterdam, to go with his suits, his butler, his Daimler, and his pet dogs. He named it Palazzo di Pietro. The house was bought by an admirer after Fortuyn's murder. Everything has been lovingly preserved. One can visit the house on a "virtual tour" at www.palazzodipietro.nl. First comes the family crest, designed by "Professor Dr. W.S.P. Fortuyn" himself, an ornate coat of arms with two stylized lions, a type of Greek goddess, and a crown topped with a pair of stag horns. A click of the mouse then guides the visitor through the marble-floored hall, the drawing room, the study, and various other rooms, all done up in a self-consciously classical style with candelabra, empire furniture, red velvet drapery, nineteenth-century paintings, and various busts and pictures of Fortuyn. A set of photographs in an album embossed with the family crest shows Fortuyn relaxing in his house in Italy, Fortuyn driving the Daimler, Fortuyn with Kenneth and Carla, Fortuyn giving a speech, and Fortuyn reclining like a movie diva in his professorial cap and gown. It is pretentious but not without humor. He took such delight in his masquerade, and yet there is that hint of travesty, the arched eyebrow, the mocking smile of the eternal outsider.

Fortuyn may have meant everything he said, but he was also a political jester, a trickster. Like all tricksters, he was driven by resentment, which was perhaps the most genuine thing about him. His own sexuality played a role, as he often admitted, but his resentments found a wider resonance, for they spoke to the grievances of the déclassé. The first people to rally around him and promote him were men who had made fortunes in ways that bought them houses and yachts, but no social cachet: the former disk jockey who became an entertainment mogul, the real estate developers, advertising men, right-wing publicists, and organizers of "events." A whiff of criminality hung over some of these men. All knew that no matter how much money they made, they would never be Our Kind of People.

Feeling socially excluded, the newly rich felt their lack of political influence. Fortuyn was their ticket to real power, or so they hoped. Raw self-interest was no doubt a part of their agenda: lower taxes, less bureaucracy, more freedom to make deals. But this was not all. Some, at least, appear to have been inspired by bigger visions, of government by businesslike strongmen who would clean up the mess of parliamentary politics once and for all. A fresh wind would invigorate a society that had been weakened for too long by wishy-washy do-gooders.

A hint of what these shadowy men are like came to me from an unusual figure in the Dutch political landscape, a genuinely conservative intellectual who had founded a think tank named after the great Irish conservative, Edmund Burke. Bart-Jan Spruyt, an intense, tweedy man in his forties, good-looking in a Nordic way, with blond hair cropped short over a bony face, wrote a book entitled *In Praise of Conservatism*.[5] His heroes include Alexis de Tocqueville and C. S. Lewis. He is a devout member of the Calvinist Church.

After the murder of Pim Fortuyn, some of his former backers approached Spruyt as a man who could be useful. They treated him to meals in expensive restaurants, feeling him out on this and that, seeing whether they might do business. In the end, they decided that a think tank was not what they were looking for. But not before they had taken Spruyt out to one more fancy restaurant. At the end of the meal, when cigars were lit and liqueurs ordered, one of the businessmen pulled out his checkbook and wrote out a check for 150,000 euros. Slipping it across the table to Spruyt, the man said: "And now get rid of those fucking Moroccans."*

---

*Spruyt did not take the money. He did, however, enter politics in a more active capacity by joining forces with Geert Wilders, a right-wing politician with an anti-immigration agenda.

I was puzzled by this story. Why the Moroccans? Lower taxes, less social welfare, these I could understand, but why would a rich businessman, who was unlikely ever to see the inside of a dish city, be so concerned about Moroccan immigrants?

So I asked Frits Bolkestein. Since he had been the first mainstream politician to voice his concern over immigration, I thought he might have the answer. He looked at me intently and said: "One must never underestimate the degree of hatred that Dutch people feel for Moroccan and Turkish immigrants. My political success is based on the fact that I was prepared to listen to such people." It was a remarkable statement, but I was still puzzled, for it didn't really answer my question. Why would a rich man feel such hatred for people who might never cross his path? This mystery goes to the heart of Fortuyn's success. He struck a nerve that went beyond personal interests.

6.

Funerals of public figures often provoke mass hysteria. It is on such occasions that you see what lurks in the hearts of millions. The outpouring of grief, though perhaps genuinely felt, can look phony. To some extent it is. The emotions are misplaced, for they are almost never based on personal acquaintance. But the dead person serves as a focus of real anxieties and disappointments. During his short career, Fortuyn knew how to manipulate popular sentiment. If his killer was fanatically principled, Fortuyn was a master of emotional kitsch.

Again, class has little to do with it. Fortuyn's funeral has been compared to that of Princess Diana, a real aristocrat who behaved like an excluded outsider, which, in a way, she was too. Some people claimed that her demise shook them up more than the death of an intimate friend, or even a husband or parent, an astonishing confession. Diana also had a natural bent for kitsch. She brought pop culture to the British monarchy and turned the institution into a soap opera. Spectacle always was part of politics, of course, monarchist or not. What Fortuyn had in common with Princess Diana was not just his embrace of showbiz as a political tool—Silvio Berlusconi, Arnold Schwarzenegger, and Ronald Reagan had done that as well—but his instinct for pop sentimentality.

Fortuyn has been compared to the popular Dutch singer André Hazes, a man with the looks and build of a long-distance truck driver and the dress sense of a 1970s lounge singer in Las Vegas: white suits, open shirts, chunky gold chains. This lachrymose wailer of songs with such titles as "Lonely Christmas," or "She Believes in Me," or "The

Kite"—about a small boy who ties a letter to his kite, destined for his mother in heaven—abused his tattooed body so
badly with drink that he died at the age of fifty-three, two
years after Fortuyn was killed.

Fifty thousand people filled the largest soccer stadium in
Amsterdam, where Hazes's coffin was displayed on the kick-
off point—the altar, as it were, in the giant open-air cathedral of popular sentiment—and thousands more stood
outside watching the events on huge screens. Job Cohen, the
Amsterdam mayor, told the masses that when Hazes wrote
his songs "he dipped his pen in his heart." The occasion was
like a religious jamboree, with much singing, mournful si-
lences, and testimonials from friends and relatives, including
the singer's ten-year-old son, who cried, "Papa, I love you!"
National radio stations played "She Believes in Me" one more
time. His ashes were blasted over the North Sea from a can-
non. The same woman who said that men like Pim Fortuyn
are born only once in a thousand years mentioned one other
example of similar rarity and eminence: André Hazes.

7.

What, then, was Fortuyn's message to the people who
adored him? What deliverance did he promise? I think
it was a nostalgic dream born of his own sense of isolation.[6]

Like many people, in France as well as in the Netherlands, who voted against the proposed constitution for the European Union in 2005, Fortuyn thought of Europe as a place without a soul, an abstraction that appealed only to top politicians, elite cultural figures, international businessmen, Our Kind of People on a European scale. In his vision, a national community should be like a family, which shares the same language, culture, and history. Foreigners who arrived with their own customs and traditions disturbed the family-state. "How dare you!" he fulminated against such aliens in one of his columns: "This is our country, and if you can't conform, you should get the hell out, back to your own country and culture."[7] What mattered in the ideal family-state wasn't class, it was "what we want to be: one people, one country, one society."

Despite his protests to the contrary, this kind of thing did put Fortuyn in the same camp as right-wing populists in other parts of Europe. Yet he came to his vision from a different angle, not the murky Nazi revanchism of Jörg Haider, or the bitterness of Jean-Marie Le Pen's memories of fighting Arabs in Algeria, but from his own sense of detachment. If he couldn't belong to any existing community, he would invent one. To establish his idealized vision of a Dutch family-state, the people would need a leader to guide them. "A leader of substance," he wrote, "is both a father and mother. . . . The capable leader is the biblical good shepherd . . . who will lead us to the father's house. Let us prepare for his coming. . . ."

In 2001, before his first electoral triumph, he gave a very peculiar interview. "Even if I don't become prime minister," he said, "I still will be. Because that is how many people see me. Politics cry out for a *turnaround*. So you have to show the people. Precisely. Politics on the spot. I will visit hospitals and schools, and I'll show the nurses and teachers exactly how to do things. . . . That is the type of leader we need. Someone who can show people what to do. Then you will automatically become the incarnation of the people."[8]

It sounds slightly deranged, those strange shifts of personal pronouns from "we" to "you" to "I." It is the fantasy of a dictatorial dreamer, the "politics on the spot," the idea of natural selection to be leader. It is the language used in the leadership cults of Kim Il Sung or Chairman Mao. What makes this most peculiar is that Fortuyn's model in this reverie was neither Mao, nor Kim, but Joop den Uyl, a former prime minister, whose brand of puritanical social democracy was not some romantic ideal, but a typical product of Dutch moralism, profoundly influenced by the Calvinist attitudes he grew up with. Den Uyl's aim to level Dutch society by taxing the wealthy was bold for its time, the early 1970s, but he was far from being a dictator, and his policies would have been loathed by Fortuyn's rich backers. But to seek for consistency here is to miss the point. Like so much else in a society that appears on the surface to have rejected the Church, Catholic or Protestant, Fortuyn's views were still steeped in biblical terms. He was the leader who, in a secular age, would guide his Dutch flock back to the father's house. What made him a potential menace was that both he and his followers imagined him to be the father—the father they had lost.

The loathing of Islam, then, may have gone deeper than a hatred of those Moroccan vandals who threatened gay men in Rotterdam. To see it as the conflict of rival monotheistic religions is too simple. Fortuyn's venom is drawn more from the fact that he, and millions of others, not just in the Netherlands, but all over Europe, had painfully wrested themselves free from the strictures of their own religions. And here were these newcomers injecting society with religion once again. The fact that many Europeans, including Fortuyn, were less liberated from religious yearnings than they might have imagined, made the confrontation with Islam all the more painful. This was especially true of those who considered themselves to be people of the Left. Some swapped the faiths of their parents for Marxist illusions, until they too ended in disillusion. The religious zeal of immigrants was a mirror image of what they themselves once had been.

Theo van Gogh's fascination with "the divine baldy" was more idiosyncratic. He certainly had no longing for a family-state, nor a hankering for a strong leader to herd the Dutch into a collective state of bliss. But he shared Fortuyn's allergy to the *regenten,* their smugness, their complacency, their patronizing air of "we know best." Both he and Fortuyn, though not quite the same age, were products of the 1960s, when the rebellion against the pillars of church and state shook everything up. To shake things up was Van Gogh's aim in life. It kept him going. Whatever else he said or did, Fortuyn shook things up in the polders of his native country. And like Van Gogh, he paid with his life.

THREE

The Healthy Smoker

"He was a bit of a moral crusader, wasn't he?" said she.

"I don't know why you should say that," he replied.

"Oh, you're all such Calvinists!" she rejoined.

"Well, I'm not sure . . ." he protested.

"Oh, yes, Theo was a Calvinist . . ."

We were sitting in the garden by the lake in Wassenaar. The pink roses were still in bloom, the rippling water was covered in white lilies. A little above where we were sitting on the gently sloping lawn, drinking tea from porcelain cups, was the large white villa, well stocked with family furniture and good books, where Theo van Gogh and his two younger sisters grew up. There was nothing marginal about this, or petit bourgeois. This was the social chic to which the likes of Pim Fortuyn could only aspire.

Theo's mother, Anneke, still a beautiful woman, with sharp blue eyes and light blond hair, wore an elegant red twinset, and had a box of cigarettes readily at hand. Johan, his father, a trim figure in slacks and an open shirt, used to work as an analyst for the secret service—a job not discussed at home. He spoke in the cultivated, discreet manner of a professional spook, leaving the faint impression that he always knew more than he was letting on. He was happy to let his wife do most of the talking.

She told me how Theo was already a rebel at primary school, where he wrote a pamphlet entitled *The Dirty Paper*. It ran to two issues. The main subject was shit and piss. His co-author was an aristocrat named Johan Quarles van Ufford. I recognized the name. Although Theo was born in 1957, five years after me, and I did not meet him until many years later, I knew the air he breathed where he grew up. The Hague has many social layers, some with very rough edges, but the town of our childhoods was a buttoned-down place of bureaucrats, bankers, and lawyers, where joining a tennis or cricket club meant being quizzed about one's grandparents' lineage, where little boys were bullied for wearing the "wrong" kind of neckties, where kids returned to school after their Christmas breaks in Switzerland with bronzed faces and broken legs, where girls wore Hermès scarves and pearl necklaces, where eighteen-year-old boys drove onto the playground in their Mini Coopers, splashing the teachers on their bicycles, and where names like Quarles van Ufford still cut a great deal of ice.

Wassenaar was a plush extension of The Hague, a verdant suburb of rolling lawns, gravel drives, and large villas, with bucolic touches like thatched roofs and stone lanterns.

Ambassadors of the larger countries had their residences in Wassenaar, alongside bankers and captains of industry, hidden from the prying gaze of hoi polloi. Its hushed, leafy streets, well-tended gardens, and sturdy gates spoke of wood-paneled discretion, of quiet evasions, of things left unsaid.

The Van Goghs, however, were not like everyone else. A rebellious streak runs though the family. Johan, the grandson of Theo, the famous artist's brother, comes from a family of strict Calvinists who mixed with socialists. His mother was a Wibaut, one of the founding families of the first Social Democratic party. Several Wibauts were in the Resistance during the war. Johan's brother, Theo, was a member of the student fraternity in Amsterdam when the war broke out. He refused to sign the loyalty oath required by the Nazis, and joined the Resistance, where, among other things, he helped to forge papers and hide Jews. In 1945, he was arrested, along with the rest of his resistance group. Shortly before the end of the war he was executed in the dunes near the North Sea.

Anneke also came from a line of socialists, but with a vicarious aristocratic pedigree. Because her grandfather worked as majordomo for one of the grander Amsterdam families, her mother was able to attend the French school with the aristocratic daughters and take piano lessons. This could have turned her into a snob, but in fact she remained firmly on the Left, as did Anneke's father, who joined the Resistance with a number of other socialists. Arrested for helping Jews and working for an underground newspaper, he spent time in a concentration camp, was freed in 1944, and immediately resumed his illegal activities. "He was relentless," Anneke explained. "He would never give up, just like Theo."

In a country where only a small number of people were active resisters, as opposed to minding their own business, this made Theo's family unusual. They were also keen members of the Society of Humanists, now a defunct institution, founded in 1947 as a kind of pillar for people who sought a spiritual life without believing in God. Instead of the Bible, they read Voltaire, the secular saint of dissident literature. Theo's grandfather made sure that Dutch soldiers had the benefit of humanist "counselors." Dutch radio on Sunday mornings used to be almost entirely devoted to sermons, given by a variety of priests and ministers. At 9:45, a humanist would hold forth about the life of the spirit without God or Jesus.

Calvinism, socialism, humanism—all left their marks. Perhaps this explains why Theo's father was not only a spook, but a man of quixotic missions, such as his resistance to the planned residency of the Dutch crown prince and his family in a particularly leafy part of Wassenaar. Why should a prince be allowed to hog so much land? So off he went, from door to door, eighty-year-old Johan, campaigning for a hopeless cause. He never gave up. It was, after all, a matter of principle.

2.

As a child, Theo couldn't have cared less about the war, or the heroics of his ancestors. When his father read him a children's story about a class that refused to go swimming after the Jewish pupils had been barred from the pool, he refused to listen. Theo was nine at the time, so this would have been in 1966, the big year of rebellion in Amsterdam, when the city was turned upside down by Provos in white jeans throwing smoke bombs at the royal coach bearing Princess (now Queen) Beatrix and her bridegroom, Prince Claus von Amsberg, a German diplomat who had joined the Hitler Youth as a schoolboy. There was nothing unusual about this; most Germans of his age had. Certainly nothing about Prince Claus suggested that he harbored any residual Nazi sympathies. Quite the contrary. But celebrating the royal wedding in Amsterdam, city of rebels and republicans, was seen as a provocation.

Provocation was what the youth rebellion was all about,* provocation of the authorities, to expose the authoritarian in-

*Hence "Provos," short for "provocateurs."

stincts of the *regenten* class, staging "happenings" and demonstrations, waiting, even hoping, for the police to reveal the heavy hand of authority. (Exposing "repressive tolerance," as Herbert Marcuse, a guru of the student Left, put it.) Similar mutinies broke out all over the world, in Paris, Prague, London, Berkeley, Berlin, Tokyo. What they had in common was youth; youth against the middle-aged. But, as with the response to political Islam, there were national differences, reflecting national histories. In Prague, the revolt was against Communist dictatorship. In Amsterdam, it was against "consumer culture," against slavery to TV and the family car, against the boredom of affluence. But this being Holland, it was also against the pillars of religious and political authority that had held society together for so long.

The revolt actually began with a television program, broadcast in 1964. I was reminded of it when a woman in her forties remarked to me one night in Amsterdam that it was, in her words, "impossible to imagine people in our culture getting violently upset over religion." (We had just been to see two Muslim actors, discovered by Theo van Gogh, perform in a theater near the mosque where Mohammed Bouyeri used to worship.) She had forgotten, or perhaps never knew about, *Zo is het toevallig ook nog'is een keer,* a satirical television program modeled after the BBC's *That Was the Week That Was.*

The presenters of *Zo is het* included various well-known

journalists, a young gay novelist, and a TV presenter named Mies Bouwman. The novelist, Gerard van het Reve, was to become famous, not just through his books, but as a more and more clownish purveyor of outrageously right-wing opinions, who converted to a kind of camp Catholicism— half Pim Fortuyn, half Oscar Wilde. A brave literary pioneer of confessional gay fiction on the one hand, and a sardonic, half-serious reactionary on the other, he preceded Van Gogh as a verbal provocateur whose extreme views and very public personal feuds were never taken entirely seriously.

But the real celebrity in the *Zo is het* team was Mies Bouwman. She had become a national star in 1962 by hosting a forty-eight-hour nonstop TV and radio charity show to open a village for physically handicapped people. *Open the Village* caused an explosion of nationwide hysteria. Every celebrity, major or minor, anyone with any name value at all, as well as a constant stream of Boy Scouts, amateur conjurers, local policemen, and guitar-playing nuns, passed through the studio for a few minutes in the spotlight with "our Mies." The sudden collective passion for "The Village" reached such a pitch that people were literally stuffing money through the gates of the television studio. I followed it on the radio. Like many people, we did not yet own a TV; my father worried that it would be bad for our minds. In a way, the radio, leaving more to the imagination, made the event even more exciting.

But *Zo is het* was pure television. Nothing dramatic happened when it started in the fall of 1963, poking mild fun at pillars of the establishment. There was the usual trickle of hate mail denouncing the "dirty Reds!" and "filthy Jews!"—nothing more. Every new program will stir up a few cranks. The third program in the series, on January 4, 1964, promised to be a little more provocative, but no one expected it to spark quite the reaction it did. It was a skit, performed by "our Mies" and the others, called *Beeldreligie,* "Screen Religion." The idea was to mock the devotion in more and more middle-class households to television. As the churches were emptying, people were basking in the luminous glow of their new house altars. Passages from the Bible, including the Ten Commandments, were read by a law student from Amsterdam, substituting the word "screen" for "God."

It was hardly outrageous, indeed it was tame compared to what a much more subversive figure like Lenny Bruce was doing around the same time in America. But the fallout was extraordinary. Newspapers cried shame on their front pages. The prime minister was furious. Questions were asked in parliament, demanding to know why the authorities hadn't prevented this outrage from being broadcast. The culture and education minister had plans to make sure that a similar program would never be aired again.

And then the letters came, thousands of them, many semiliterate: Dirty Reds! Filthy Jews! of course, but also: "It may take time, but one day we'll ram you with our car. It's dark where you live. You've had your time." Or this: "One of these days we'll get you NSBers [Nazi collaborators]* and Jews. We'll get you, you filthy gang. . . . You should have become a pimp [sic] . . ." Or this, showing a peculiar degree of historical confusion: "After liberation from Germany we shaved the hair off the hated NSBers, now we'll come and shave that hated bunch who made that shameful program, we'll bring the necessary pots of tar, as well as bottles of petrol and hydrochloric acid. . . ."

NSBers were the Dutch Nazis. The rigid insistence after the war to brand people in hindsight as "good" or "bad," patriots or traitors, anti-Nazis or NSBers, was a sign perhaps of high moral principle. More likely it was a reflection of the guilty conscience of a people who had been, on the whole, neither wholly good nor wholly bad. More disturbing is the fact that in 1964, "Jews" was used as an insult along with "NSBers." That some of the anonymous writers appear not to have known the difference is perhaps most disturbing of all. "Our Mies," denounced as a "Jewish whore," was in fact a Catholic. For some people, "Jewish," like "NSBer," had

*NSB standing for "Nationaal Socialistische Beweging," the Dutch National Socialist Party.

clearly become a term for anything rotten. Mies's children needed police escorts to go to school. Herman Wigbold, the producer, needed day and night protection.

But the pillars were tottering. With the Beatles and the Rolling Stones, the home-grown Provos and the Pill, they began to fall. Amsterdam was the center of the revolt. The Provos, in white denim, were both rebellious and utopian. *Homo ludens* would rule in New Babylon. White bicycles were distributed around the city for anyone to hop onto. Plans were made to feed LSD into the Amsterdam waterworks, or laughing gas into the church where the royal wedding would take place. A monument to Lieutenant General J. B. van Heutsz, a former governor general of the Dutch East Indies, became a popular place for demonstrations. In 1965, it was defaced with white paint. In 1967, it was smashed by a homemade bomb.

Van Heutsz was not a random target. In a country with no war heroes to speak of since the seventeenth century, when Admirals Tromp and De Ruyter defeated the British fleet, Van Heutsz was regarded as a hero in the second decade of the twentieth century for crushing Muslim resistance against Dutch colonial rule in Atjeh. He accomplished this feat with extraordinary brutality. Women and children were executed, and countless people tortured. The Dutch war against the Atjeh jihadis cost more than a hundred thousand lives. Nonetheless, a large monument was erected in 1935, designed by a Communist sculptor. The NSB was happy to pay tribute to a true Dutch hero. Van Heutsz's son, J. B. van Heutsz, Jr., later joined the SS.

The monument was attacked by the Provos just as the veil over the dark side of Dutch history was beginning to be lifted. The first serious study of the Holocaust in the Netherlands, J. Presser's *The Downfall,* was published in 1965. My history teacher, an amiable storyteller much loved by his pupils, happened to have been a former NSBer. It was odd, thinking back, that so little was made of this. After all, where I lived, everyone knew that one didn't buy meat from a certain butcher, since the old man had been "wrong" during the war, or cigarettes from the lady who had had a German lover. We had no idea whether these allegations were true. But we still shunned these people, as though their tainted pasts were contagious.

Dear Mr. Veenhoven, at any rate, didn't teach us Nazi propaganda, so far as I can remember. But when the social-ist television channel (pillars were tottering, but still alive) broadcast a program about the "excesses" of Dutch soldiers in their futile but bloody attempt to crush Indonesian inde-pendence, our teacher could not contain his rage. In class the next morning, he fumed against the program's producers: "Those red traitors . . ." Now Veenhoven was a somewhat unusual man, but he was by no means alone in his reaction. And this was in 1969, five years after *Zo is het* and the beginning of Provo.

Then again, where Theo van Gogh and I grew up, things did tend to happen late. Provo was really an Amsterdam phenomenon. Harry Mulisch, the famous novelist, who wrote a book about Provo, even described it as an Amsterdam revolt against the provinces. While the long-haired kids in white jeans were attacking the Van Heutsz monument, while the students of Paris barricaded the Left Bank, while Prague had its Spring, and everyone, from London to Tokyo, was protesting against the Vietnam War, we too held a demonstration in our schoolyard. The headmaster, a very conservative gentleman, had, after careful consideration and due consultation with the parents, decided that the nineteenth-century spelling of our school's name should be updated. Nederlandsch Lyceum would henceforth be simplified to Nederlands Lyceum. This, for us pupils of this venerable institution, was a step too far. And so we stood firm, in our blazers and pearls and Hermès scarves, shouting in brave defiance: *"Nederlandsch, Nederlandsch, S–C–H . . . S–C–H . . . S–C–H!"*

And still the war cast its pall everywhere—everywhere, that is, except in our history class, or perhaps even there, because of what was left unsaid. The war was not just reflected in the absurd invective of hate-mail writers. Provo was under the same spell. And so were other dissidents in the land of the *regenten*. Amsterdam was run by a city council dominated by nice Social Democrats. The mayor, who would preside over the royal wedding, was a member of the PVDA. But when the Amsterdam police charged into demonstrators with truncheons, they were jeered as the "Orange SS," or, in the words of Harry Mulisch, the "Gestapo in clogs." Claus von Amsberg, the prince-to-be, a man of known liberal disposition, was greeted by crowds of young protesters shouting "Clauschwitz."

It was as if the postwar generation needed to make up for the failure of their parents. The sons and daughters of those who had been unable to prevent a hundred thousand Jews from being singled out for murder would fight the new dictators, the Orange SS, the Gestapo in clogs, the German diplomat who had joined the Hitler Youth as a child. There was something pathetic about this belated show of resistance, but also telling. The nation of Anne Frank had not come to terms with its recent and most dramatic past, not with the German occupation, and not with what happened in Indonesia either. The suggestion that the *regenten* who governed the Netherlands, let alone Amsterdam, were in any way comparable to the Nazis was typical of this. It was doubly unfortunate, for using the Occupation as a polemical

tool was a distortion that not only diminished the importance of historical guilt, but also of the bravery of those who
did risk their lives to help strangers.

3.

A Saturday afternoon, sometime in the early 1990s. My
friend Hans had got us two tickets for the Ajax-
Feyenoord game at the old Olympic Stadium in Amsterdam.
This was always an event fraught with mob emotion, even violence. Amsterdam versus Rotterdam; the capital against
"the peasants"; the city of arts and culture against the city of
honest toilers; Mokum, the erstwhile Jewish city, against the
Dutch salt of the earth. These are the clichés in which urban
rivalries trade.

Soccer partisanship is often rooted in ethnicity. Many
European capitals—Berlin, Budapest, London, Vienna—had
clubs that were once associated with a Jewish following,
and these legacies die hard, even when there is no more fac-
tual basis for them. Ajax had had a fair number of Jewish
members before the war, but most of them were killed.
There were a few Jewish Ajax players after the war, but not
enough to make a difference. Nonetheless, just as postwar
Amsterdam still had several Jewish mayors, Ajax still had
Jewish owners, at least some of the time. The phantom of

Mokum still haunts the city, and has been given a strange new lease on life in the soccer stadium.

After Provo and the first critical discussions of the Holocaust, to be Jewish in some Dutch circles became rather chic. At least until the Yom Kippur War in 1973, Israel was widely admired. And Israelis still warmed their hearts with the myth of the gallant Dutch who stood up for the Jews in their darkest hour, of the doughty Amsterdam workers who, uniquely in occupied Europe, went on strike in protest against the Jewish deportations. The strike had indeed taken place, in February 1941. It was inspiring, even though it did no good. At a time, decades later, when people would rather not think about the past at all, it could still produce a spark of pride.

This spark went into the mystique of the great Ajax teams of the 1970s. Something in the freedom of their play, the swagger of their "total football," was attributed to the urban myth of Mokum. The fans from rival cities sensed this and began to refer to Ajax as "the Jews," or rather "the rotten Jews," "the cancer Jews," "the filthy Jews." This had little or nothing to do with ancestry, or with the war. Every supporter of the "Jew club" had to be a "Jew." Things began to escalate from there. The more supporters from Rotterdam, Utrecht, or The Hague cried "Jew!" the more the myth of Mokum, and by extension Israel, was evoked. By the 1980s, Ajax fans turned up in their stadium wrapped in Stars of David and the Israeli flag.

When Hans and I arrived at the Olympic Stadium, it was soon clear that a terrible mistake had been made. Hans was an Ajax supporter, but through some unfortunate error our tickets put us in the middle of the Feyenoord block. This meant that we had better keep our heads down. Things were already getting heated at the gates. Cops on horseback tried to keep the supporters in line with truncheons and sticks. Thousands of men, rowdy from drinking beer since the early morning, had to be pressed through one tiny gate. "Fucking Jews!" they shouted as they were being herded toward the stands.

"Fucking Jews!" they went again every time an Ajax player touched the ball, even if he was a black Surinamese. "Cancer Jew!" they shouted when the blond referee from the northern province of Friesland whistled for a Feyenoord foul. And then I heard it for the first time, a sinister hissing sound from hundreds, maybe thousands, of beer-flecked mouths. I didn't know what it meant, until Hans explained it. The sound got louder: the sound of escaping gas. In Budapest soccer stadiums, players of a side owned by a Jewish businessman were greeted by rival supporters shouting: "The trains to Auschwitz are ready!" In the Olympic Stadium of Amsterdam, the fans were a touch more inventive.

4.

When he was thirteen, Theo van Gogh was taken, much against his will, to a cemetery in Overveen, a place in the dunes on the North Sea, where the Germans took their political prisoners to be executed. Commemorating the war dead on May 4, an annual Dutch ritual, had always filled him with embarrassment, perhaps even disgust, for these occasions reduced his father to tears. The only person who could talk to Theo about the war without causing embarrassment was his maternal grandfather, whom he adored. Theo visited him many times in the hospital before the old man died in 1967. The trip to Overveen, however, turned out to be meaningful after all. For there among the names of the resisters was that of his uncle Theo, which impressed him deeply. Soon he was reading everything he could about the war.

He also became increasingly hard to handle. Theo always was an eccentric child. Standing in the garden giving loud speeches to "my fellow countrymen" was certainly odd. And making a short film on 8mm of his friends eating excrement (simulated by pulped gingersnaps) was mildly unusual. But his desire to shock, to stir things up in the sleepy suburbs, escalated. When he set off firecrackers in the classroom, he was forced to find another school.

Much had changed even in the four years since I had left

school in The Hague. And not everything Theo did was designed to outrage. He ran a helpline for classmates who had bad trips on LSD. This turned into a battle of wills with his headmaster. Theo refused to back down. At home, he argued endlessly with his parents, dominated every conversation, smashed the neighbors' windows, and drank his father's best wines in all-night parties with his friends. None of this was criminal behavior, more the manner of a bored Wassenaar brat. Theo's favorite movie was Stanley Kubrick's *A Clockwork Orange,* about a gang of ultra-violent teenagers. By the time he finished high school, his mother had had enough and told him to leave home.

Now I sat with his parents on the same lawn where Theo had once addressed his fellow countrymen, in the shade of a large oak tree, and moved on from afternoon tea to a fine dry rosé. "He was always different," said Anneke, her eyes brimming with affection, "always going against the grain." When the hippie fads of the early 1970s had reached even Wassenaar, most of Theo's friends traveled to Nepal or India. But not Theo. He went to the United States. "Theo always loved America," said his mother, "even when it was not popular at all. He adored it. New York!"

In Amsterdam, where he claims never to have felt at home, Theo led a drifting bohemian life, drinking, doing drugs, sleeping at different addresses, always in the safe knowledge that he could return to Wassenaar on the weekends, his bags filled with laundry. He applied twice to the film academy, submitting a short film about a master stabbed in the eyes with the stem of a wineglass by his vengeful slave, and was told to go and see a psychiatrist. After trying and failing to be a law student, he got work as a stage manager. Then, in 1981, with the help of friends and rich Wassenaar contacts, he made his first film. *Luger* was a black farce about the kidnapping of a millionaire's wheelchair-bound daughter. The film received some attention, not least because of two remarkable scenes, one of which shows a man shoot off his gun into a woman's vagina, and another where the same man stuffs two cats into a washing machine. He went on to make twenty-three more films. Some, such as *A Day on the Beach* (1984), *Blind Date* (1996), and *Interview* (2003), have been acclaimed for their boldness and originality. Van Gogh worked fast, with several cameras at the same time. And he was good with actors. This gave a freshness to his best work, but often he was in too much of a hurry, as though he were terrified he would crash if he stood still.

Although he came of age only in the 1970s, Van Gogh was still a provocative child of the 1960s, an heir of the Provos. But at the same time, he was part of the reaction, of the rebellion against the rebellion. One of the reasons soccer hooligans from Rotterdam called their Amsterdam counterparts "filthy Jews" was ignorance. Another, possibly more compelling reason was that it was the most shocking thing one could say in post-Holocaust Europe. They may not have realized quite why, but the hooligans knew they were breaking a taboo. They were shouting something out loud that respectable people would not even have dared to mutter under their breath, especially in the 1960s, when the Jewish genocide got widespread attention for the first time.

Something of that sort may have driven Theo van Gogh, not at all an ignorant man, to abuse a number of Dutch Jews. It was never easy to get funding for independent films in Holland, so perhaps his attacks on contemporaries such as Leon de Winter, a filmmaker and novelist, were partly inspired by jealousy. When De Winter, the son of orthodox Jewish parents, had some success with stories inspired by his family background, he was accused by Theo of using his Jewishness for self-promotion, of getting rich by shedding fake tears. In a movie magazine entitled *Moviola*, Theo wrote that De Winter could only satisfy his wife by wrapping barbed wire around his penis and crying "Auschwitz!" when he came. De Winter's alleged sentimentality was ridiculed in visions of diabetic Jews being gassed, giving off the smell of caramel. "Yellow stars copulating in the gas chambers" was another line in the same piece.

A young Jewish academic named Evelien Gans described Theo's attacks on De Winter as "theme envy." Theo immediately lashed out against her too. Gans, he wrote, "gets wet dreams about being fucked by Dr. Mengele," the Auschwitz doctor. De Winter later lamented that only a few Jews bothered to complain about Van Gogh's remarks. In fact, Van Gogh was sued by the Centre for Information and Documentation on Israel. The case dragged on for years. It went to the supreme court. Van Gogh accused his judges of being corrupted by Jewish money. He was found guilty, only to get in trouble again by insisting on republishing the offending articles in a collection. This time, somewhat inconsistently, the courts upheld his right to do so. He went on and on, publishing the same stuff. He would never give up.

The Jews were not the only ones to feel Theo's fury. Irate Christians took him to court for calling Jesus Christ "that rotten fish from Nazareth." Sometimes the invective was just personal. His oldest friend, Thom Hoffman, who acted in Theo's first film before going on to work with more commercial directors, was publicly denounced as a "walking tube of Vaseline." A well-known actress who mourned the death of her child was ridiculed for "making a career out of her grief." Various politicians and public figures who crossed him were told to die slowly of terrible diseases. Mayor Cohen was called a collaborating mayor under the Nazis. And so on, and on, until the Muslims attracted his particular scorn and were subjected to a constant barrage of abuse, of which "goat fuckers" was the most quoted but by no means most offensive example.

Despite being a huge celebrity in a small country, with

columns and personal appearances in pretty much every newspaper, magazine, and television program at one time or another, Van Gogh always craved more attention. It was not enough to be a well-regarded filmmaker. He had a permanent hunger for publicity. Perhaps his personal attacks were inspired less by theme envy than attention envy. He did not like others to get into his limelight. His problem, as a columnist and TV personality, was that he rarely lasted anywhere for long without being shown the door. His last, and perhaps most widely read, column, *The Healthy Smoker*, appeared on his own website, theovangogh.nl, and in *Metro*, a free paper handed out on trains.

There was, however, another side to his character. He could be a gracious host, always insisting on picking up the tab in restaurants, or, perhaps a little too ostentatiously, ordering rounds of champagne at the bar. But his best quality was his curiosity. This made him a receptive, indeed generous interviewer, asking probing questions without imposing his own views. As a guest on one of his television shows, I was so seduced by his good manners and intelligent interest that I quite forgot about the vile cold I was nursing. But I saw the other Theo, too, when we were both on a radio show hosted by his friend Max Pam. One of the other guests was a quiet-spoken museum curator in a dark suit, who had just put on a huge exhibition of Mondrian paintings. "Wasn't this a typical example of arrogant elitism?" asked Theo. Who wanted to see so much abstract art? Shouldn't popular taste be taken more seriously? "Well," said the man, very politely, "perhaps the public should be educated . . ." He wasn't able to finish his sentence. "Educated?" Who the fuck was he to . . . Fucking elitist crap! Get out of here! And so on, without relent. The curator looked crushed. I stared at the floor. Pam looked content. Good show. Typical Theo.

The design of *The Healthy Smoker* tells us as much about Van Gogh as the website of the Palazzo di Pietro does about Pim Fortuyn. The contrast could not be greater. If Fortuyn was all piss-elegant classicism, Van Gogh's style was all adolescent outrage, very much in the spirit, in fact, of the *Dirty Paper* of his primary schooldays. The first thing you see is a color photograph of Van Gogh wearing a red bra over his eyes, and then a coat of arms showing three swords and a slack pink penis above the words *Luctor et Emergo*, "I Shall Struggle and Stand Up." If Fortuyn was a preening dandy, Van Gogh made a show of his unwashed, disheveled, overweight ugliness: the huge pink belly straining under old T-shirts, the nicotine-stained teeth, the nose picking, the scratching, the general disdain for personal hygiene. Fortuyn aspired to class; Van Gogh played his own class down.

Van Gogh clearly saw the endless feuds and tirades as part of his lifelong struggle, but for what? The personal element is perhaps most easily explained. He could be a loyal friend, but demanded total loyalty in exchange. The slightest lapse, or perception of a lapse, was seen as a betrayal, and led to total war. That is why Thom Hoffman, an early comrade-in-arms against the commercial film industry, could not be forgiven for joining it. He had to remain a comrade, a fellow outsider, a man of principled opposition, a resister. If not, he was the enemy.

Friends of Theo claim that even his most unreasonable behavior was often inspired by a sense of principle. Max Pam: "Passion, loyalty, honesty, and principled behavior, these were things that Theo demanded from himself, but also from the people around him. As soon as he suspected cowardice or hypocrisy, that person was beyond the pale."[1]

The insistence on total frankness, the idea that tact is a form of hypocrisy, and that everything, no matter how sensitive, should be stated openly, with no holds barred, the elevation of bluntness to a kind of moral ideal; this willful lack of delicacy is a common trait in Dutch behavior. Perhaps its roots are in Protestant pietism, a reaction to what was seen as glib Catholic hypocrisy. Private confession had to become public. Discretion was a sign of holding back the truth, of dishonesty. Whether it is a national trait or not, Theo van Gogh exemplified it. It explains his cruelty, but also his passion for free speech, and his defense of those whose freedoms he felt were being threatened.

Ayaan Hirsi Ali excited his sympathy when she was attacked for her hostile views of Islam. It was not so much what she said; it was the fact that people wished to prevent her from saying it. One very public thing she did, in a television documentary, was to press the twelve-year-old pupils of an Islamic school to declare their principal loyalty. Which would they choose, Allah or the Dutch constitution? It was a leading question, and of course they opted for Allah, which filled her with visible annoyance. Her point was serious. She explained that intolerance of homosexuals and Jews, as professed in the Koran, was incompatible with the equality enshrined in the constitution. But her strident tone put people off. The critical reactions were swift and often as misguided as her question. Jacques Wallage, Social Democratic mayor of Groningen, the son of Jewish survivors, claimed that Ayaan Hirsi Ali was provoking violence. She should be stopped from venting her antagonistic views of Islam in public. People should be reminded of past intolerance. Much of the Jewish community in Groningen, he said, had been wiped out during the war. Which was true enough, but perhaps not entirely relevant to this discussion.

Van Gogh's defense of Hirsi Ali was in his usual belligerent mode. Ayaan, he said, had to be surrounded by bodyguards because "thousands of followers of that backward culture called Islam think she should be eradicated for being the whore of Babylon." Wallage, "who thinks that her opinions create a climate that only existed in Groningen when Jewish children were deported, would also be happy if she were shot. . . ." A typically low blow. Van Gogh was right in one respect, however: Hirsi Ali may have been wrong to harangue those schoolgirls, but she was far from behaving like a Nazi. But then Van Gogh used the war to sink in his own poisoned dagger: "If the blessings of Allah should lead to Islamic rule in the Netherlands, Wallage will be the first one to be asked to collaborate with the occupiers in the name of the Jewish Council."[2]

Once more, it was back to the war, the deportations, collaboration. Back and forth it goes, in the land of guilty memories, where current affairs keep on taking on the colors of the past. If Leon de Winter or Jacques Wallage could be faulted for bringing up Jewish suffering even when it is beside the point, Van Gogh used Jewish suffering against the Jews in a way that was not just irrelevant but vicious. He never used the wartime heroism of his own family to score points, but he was still possessed by the Dutch obsession with "good" or "bad," traitor or resister. And he did so in a way that was sometimes far from scrupulous.

5.

Theo van Gogh's enthusiasms, apart from Stanley Kubrick's *A Clockwork Orange*, included Louis-Ferdinand Céline and the Marquis de Sade, literary taboo-breakers, bad boys who shouted out the unmentionable and the obscene. But his polemics were also in a Dutch literary tradition that goes back at least to the late nineteenth century. The writings of critics such as Lodewijk van Deyssel (1864–1952) were called *scheldkritieken,* literally "abusive criticism." Personal abuse was elevated to a high style, to be taken seriously as literature. These tirades had the added piquancy that the protagonists were bound to know each other. Holland is a small place, and the world of literature even smaller. Stylized abuse was an effective way to ritualize animosities in a tight circle. It was serious, but never deadly.

The masters of literary abuse in the twentieth century were the novelists Gerard van het Reve, who took part in *Zo is het,* and W. F. Hermans. Both had to fight off lawsuits for insulting religion, Hermans in 1952 and Van het Reve in 1966. Hermans wrote a novel in which one of the characters calls Catholics "the filthiest, creepiest, most deluded, treacherous part of our nation. But they fuck away! They reproduce! Like rabbits, rats, fleas, lice. And they don't emigrate!" Hermans told the court that these sentiments belonged to a fictional character and that literature should be free. He won his case.

Gerard van het Reve fell afoul of a blasphemy law drafted in 1932 when some Communists had argued for the abolition of Christmas. Under the new law, "scornful blasphemy" would be forbidden. Van het Reve wrote that God was a donkey, and he would make sweet love to the animal, making sure it wouldn't get hurt when it climaxed. God, he also wrote, would masturbate when thinking of Van het Reve's devotion. As always with him, the irony was laid on with such a thick brush that no one could be sure how seriously he meant to be taken. It was his tragedy to be laughed at when he was serious and attacked when he wasn't. His case made it all the way to the supreme court before it was dismissed. Van het Reve's blasphemy was judged not to have been "scornful."

Theo van Gogh placed himself squarely in the tradition of abusive criticism. Hermans was one of his heroes. When Van Gogh called Muslims "goat fuckers," or a "fifth column," or when he spun fantasies around Leon de Winter's sex life or likened Jesus to a "rotten fish," he thought he was doing what Hermans and Van het Reve had done. He was, in his own words, the national "village idiot," the fat jester with a license to tell the truth. He knew that people didn't enjoy being abused, but not in his wildest dreams did he suspect that they would kill him for it. This was the crowning irony of his life. Van Gogh, more than anyone, had warned about the dangers of violent religious passions, and yet he behaved as though they held no consequences for him. He made the mistake of assuming that the wider world would not intrude on his Amsterdam scene, with its private ironies, its personal feuds, and its brutal mockery that was never intended to draw more than imaginary blood.

6.

It was always going to be a strange debate, at the City Theatre in Amsterdam. Organized by a group of Amsterdam students and journalists called Happy Chaos, the spectacle would feature Dyab Abou Jahjah, the Belgian founder of the European-Arab League, and a Dutch Social Democrat politician named Boris Dittrich. The debate was going to be moderated by Theo van Gogh and a movie starlet named Georgina Verbaan. The topics of the debate would be feminism, idealism, and Muslim values.

There is not much to be said about Georgina Verbaan. Abou Jahjah, however, is an interesting figure. Born in a Lebanese village in 1971, he moved to Belgium in 1990, claiming that he was threatened by the Baath Party, and studied political science at Louvain. After marrying a local woman, he became a Belgian citizen, and they were divorced three months later. He founded the European-Arab League in 2000. His model was Malcolm X. Just as Malcolm did, Abou Jahjah opposes assimilation. He would like Arabs to live like Arabs in Europe, with their own political parties and schools.

Jort Kelder, editor of a glossy magazine about money and lifestyle, Georgina Verbaan's lover, and part-time actor in one of Van Gogh's films, told me what happened that night, in June 2003. Abou Jahjah entered the theater, surrounded by fierce-looking bodyguards. When told that Van Gogh would be the moderator, he refused to join the debate. Van Gogh told the audience what had happened and declared his surprise that this "pimp of the Prophet" should need the protection, not just of Allah, but of bodyguards as well. Abou Jahjah and his guards left the hall, whereupon Van Gogh urged the audience to shout "Allah knows best! Allah knows best!" Dittrich, the politician, called Van Gogh "a rude prick." Van Gogh called Dittrich "an unctuous lubricant" (Dittrich is openly gay). It was another balmy night in Amsterdam.

Outside the theater, one of the organizers was threatened by Abou Jahjah's bodyguards. When Theo walked into the fray, he was accosted by several youths of Moroccan origin. Precisely what they said is not clear. According to some witnesses, they shouted that they would "not let the fat pig get away with this." Jort Kelder heard them say "We'll get that fat pig and cut him open." Van Gogh was urged to take a taxi home. Nonsense, he said, and got on his bike.

"It was then," said Kelder, "that I realized how deeply they hated him. For us, it was just a game, a debating game. For them it was deadly serious."

Van Gogh called Kelder later and was clearly happy with the way the evening had gone. He loved a good row, and knew it would be widely reported in the papers. He would write about it himself in *The Healthy Smoker*. And yet, even though he claimed not to feel in any personal danger, something had alarmed him enough to call Ayaan Hirsi Ali on that same night, on her cell phone. She was in a taxi in New York City, driven by a Muslim driver chewing on a potent weed called *khat,* popular in Yemen and Somalia. Van Gogh was in a state of great excitement, cursing the Muslims and the cowardice of the Dutch authorities, and the danger of men like Abou Jahjah. Even when she explained that this was not the best time to talk, he wouldn't stop. They *had* to meet in Amsterdam, he said. She said she would come and see him.

FOUR

A Dutch Tragedy

1.

Najib delivered pizzas. Not that scootering around The Hague delivering pizzas was his real ambition. A bright young man of Moroccan descent, Najib spoke fluent French and English as well as his native Dutch, and dreamed of going to the university, making something of himself, being a success.

Najib's father was in bad health, ruined by too many years of hard factory work. He could barely walk anymore and sat at home watching Arab TV channels and cursing the Jews and other infidels. His mother, dressed from head to toe in black, wailed in Berber about her children who didn't understand her, her husband who beat her, and the awful fate of being stuck among strangers far from her native village in the Rif mountains. Najib's sister, Hafidah, wore jeans and a headscarf, and watched Lebanese pop groups on MTV. Najib spoke Dutch to his sister and Berber to his parents.

Julia was a pretty young Dutch girl, rich, spoiled, privileged. She had hoped to be selected for the national field hockey team. Her trainer, Floris, a callow young man with lanky blond hair, was in love with her. She was not in love with Floris. Both lived in large houses in an expensive part of The Hague, the kind of verdant suburb where the main sounds of summer are the plock of tennis balls, the tinkling of teacups, and the quiet hiss of lawn sprinklers—a world away from the concrete "dish city" that was home to Najib.

Floris's and Julia's fathers, both policemen who had married above their station, had been best friends for a long time. Their wives had money and the superior attitudes of The Hague's upper bourgeoisie. Julia's father, Albert, had once been a coarse but good-looking man, whose air of proletarian toughness might have enticed her mother, Eefje, into an ill-considered marriage. A life of unearned comfort had turned Albert into a fat, ill-mannered slob, resentful of his wife's intellect and class. Eefje found refuge from her youthful folly in a succession of New Age fads and meditations, and by tending to her rose garden.

Floris's mother had died, leaving her husband, Joost, with a fortune. Joost was a loud man in flashy clothes, who drove expensive cars, kept a large yacht, and drank too much. His late wife must also, like Eefje, have had a taste for rough masculinity. But as with Albert, this quality had turned rancid long ago.

One day, Najib saw Julia in a clothing store, where he had been harassed by a shopgirl who accused him of stealing. After all, she said, all "fucking Moroccans" are thieves. Najib kept his cool and handled the situation with dignity. Julia liked the look of him. One thing led to another; telephone messages were exchanged, dates made.

Floris was furious and assaulted Najib in the street, pushing him off his scooter and kicking him when he was down. Albert, Julia's father, tried everything to stop his daughter from seeing Najib. Joost offered to help his friend. Both wanted Floris to marry Julia—hockey coach and star player, son and daughter of wealth, blond and brunette, Dutch and Dutch.

Najib did more than deliver pizzas. Once a month, he would visit a shady character to collect money for his family. This arrangement went through Najib's brother, Nasr, who was in prison for dealing drugs. Najib had no idea where the money came from and didn't really want to know. The family needed the cash and he was saving up for university tuition.

Najib continued to see Julia despite opposition from her family and, once they heard about it, from his own too. Najib's mother was terrified that he would behave like his elder sister and run off with an infidel. When her husband found out about Najib and Julia, he went into a rage and beat his wife. Najib's younger sister, stuck between traditional family obligations and MTV-fed fantasies, was envious, as well as disapproving, of her brother.

Violence invited more violence. Floris attacked Najib again. Najib beat up Floris. Joost secretly took pictures of Najib and pretended to Julia that they were from police files. The only one to show any sympathy for the young couple was Julia's mother, who liked the young man's nice manners and the fact that he spoke French. But she was mostly lost in a haze of her own discontents and was not much good to her daughter. Things became even more complicated when Joost discovered that Najib was Nasr's brother.

Joost knew Nasr. He was getting a cut from the same Colombian gangsters who were paying Najib. Nasr, a police informer as well as a small-time drug dealer, knew all about Joost, too. In exchange for the cash supplied to his family, Nasr had agreed to serve his time in prison and keep silent. Najib's involvement with Julia threatened the whole arrangement. Najib might easily find out. Despite all this, he and Julia continued to see each other.

Joost's drinking got out of hand, and his behavior became erratic. Certain unpleasant facts began to leak out. When Albert discovered his friend's involvement with gangsters, he wanted to arrest the Colombians, and promised to protect Nasr by transferring him to another prison. In exchange he pressed him to stop his brother from seeing Julia. Nasr refused. Albert entered Nasr's cell and kicked him around so badly that he fell into a coma, and died in the hospital.

Najib's family blamed their misfortunes on Julia. Najib still loved her, but felt torn between conficting loyalties. Joost, meanwhile, tried to escape from the Colombians; he went into hiding, but was found by one of the gangsters, who hanged him. It was made to look like a suicide.

Floris blamed Najib for his father's death. The showdown took place on Joost's yacht. They fought. Najib fell into the water. He couldn't swim. Floris refused to save him.

Julia's family wouldn't allow Julia to attend Najib's funeral. Albert, in a last attempt to regain his daughter's love, showed his police badge and forced Najib's family to let her see her lover's dead body. Julia seemed to have forgiven her father, but she left her comfortable home, headed for the beach, and kept walking into the cold waves of the North Sea until she disappeared forever.

2.

This Dutch melodrama was shown on television in thirteen parts during the winter of 2002. Justus van Oel, who wrote the script, had wanted his contemporary Romeo and Juliet tale to end on a more hopeful note. The two mothers, Najib's and Julia's, would meet and console one another for the loss of their children. Through their tragic deaths, a kind of reconciliation would be possible. One day, surely, Muslims and Christians, Dutch and Moroccans, would learn to live in peace, and perhaps even love one another. But Theo van Gogh, the director, had other ideas. It had to end with death. "For him," said Justus van Oel, "it was war. The message he wanted to bang home was the total impossibility of living in peace with devout Muslims. . . . The series had to end badly, in every detail. There was no room for hope."[1]

And yet Van Gogh was more complicated than that. Although he hated Islam as much as Christianity, and thought that religion itself was the source of all evil, he also said "there are a hundred thousand decent Muslims, to whom we Dutch people ought to reach out." Although his multicultural soap opera ended badly, his sympathy was clearly with Najib and Julia, and Najib's sister, who fled to France with her non-Muslim lover. Van Gogh supported anyone—in life or in fiction—who defied conventions, who rebelled against social and religious constraints. Whatever else he was, Van Gogh was no racist.

He was one of the very few Dutch directors to make films about immigrants. And, though often provocative, he enjoyed engaging with Muslims. *Najib and Julia* was a unique effort on Dutch, or indeed European, television. In a joint enterprise with Forum, an organization that promotes multiculturalism, Van Gogh used the series to stimulate debates, about religion, sex, tolerance, and so on, in schools and other public places. Two years after making the series, he made a film called *Cool!* about juvenile delinquents at Glen Mills, an experimental reform school. Many of the actors were student/inmates, mostly Moroccan-Dutch, although the most villainous character is a pasty-faced Dutch boy who speaks in an upper-class Hague accent. Two former Glen Mills pupils, Fouad Mourigh and Farhane el-Hamchaoui, used this opportunity and became professional actors, touring the country with a play of their own, about their life in the streets as petty criminals and their redemption.

3.

I was taken to see Fouad and Farhane perform by two of the most prominent Friends of Theo: his main scriptwriter, Theodor Holman, and his producer, Gijs van de Westelaken. We drove to the theater in Gijs's convertible, speeding through the narrow nineteenth-century streets of south Amsterdam on a warm evening in June. Holman, a chunky man in his early fifties, is famous for his confessional columns and radio shows, in which he talks a great deal about his late friend Theo, as well as his own frustrations, often of a sexual nature. The theater was located in a gleaming new "community center," designed by the city authorities to foster multicultural tolerance through the arts in a heavily Muslim area that had become notorious for its high crime rate. Mohammed Bouyeri, Van Gogh's killer, was born a few streets away.

As we entered "dish city," Theodor joked about being assassinated. "I need a disguise!" he cried in mock fear. Moroccan youths, he said, often taunted him by shouting "Mohammed B. Mohammed B!" There were not many people in the streets of this dreary 1950s neighborhood. The travel agents offering cheap flights to Morocco and Turkey were closed. A few young men hung around a shabby-looking kebab joint, speaking loudly in a Dutch slang that owes much to American rap. Women in black headscarves carried plastic bags from a local supermarket. Two old men in beards and djellabas sat on a bench staring ahead in silence. From a distance the community center reminded me of a mosque, with a white minaret. It turned out to have been a Christian church before its current incarnation.

Theodor greeted the pretty young woman behind the bar, the manager of the community center, with effusive enthusiasm. Her parents were from Turkey, he explained. She had voted for Ayaan Hirsi Ali, the only one in her family and circle of friends to have done so. Theodor had tried to seduce her on several occasions, but to no avail. In the bar, he spoke gloomily of the 1960s, and how he felt "all screwed up" by the sexual liberalism of his parents. I looked around, curious to see who came to this community center. Even though we were in the middle of "dish city," few people looked non-European. The "Turkish" woman confirmed this. "Most of the locals who come here," she said, "are Dutch natives."

This was certainly true of the audience for Fouad and Farhane's play: well-meaning liberals watching two former street kids act out their road to redemption. The short play consisted of sketches, performed at great speed, of robbing old ladies at a cash machine, of neighborhood fights, of gang-banging girls, of smoking dope, of getting arrested, of being imprisoned, and finally of seeing the light, returning to school, and "doing something positive for the community."

Fouad and Farhane had performed their play at schools, in prisons, even for Job Cohen, the Amsterdam mayor. It was perhaps a little too wholesome, smacking too much of do-goodery, to be wholly satisfying as theater. But when they joined us for a soft drink at the bar afterward, there was something about them that was more intriguing, an edge that was lacking in their play. They had attitude. I wanted to hear more about their lives, but this was not the time or place. There was a lot of good-natured joshing, slapping of hands, and kidding around between them and the Friends of Theo, but little conversation. Gijs in his expensive suede shoes looked less incongruous in the community center than Fouad and Farhane in their T-shirts, baggy pants, and baseball caps.

I made a date with Farhane to meet him in The Hague, our hometown. After the two actors had left, Theodor and Gijs swapped anecdotes about Theo, about his success with women, his flowery letters full of clichés about eternal love, about his sense of irony. "Irony," said Theodor rather solemnly, "is such an essential part of the Dutch makeup. I really notice this after Theo's death. It's so much part of our tradition."

It is indeed part of the tradition, and a great deal of humor depends on it. But there is a less positive side to this tradition. Irony can be a healthy antidote to dogmatism, but also an escape from any blame. Outrageous or offensive statements are often followed by protestations that they were meant in jest, but only once their poisoned darts have hit their marks. Irony is a great license for irresponsibility. Theo van Gogh liked to call himself the village idiot, as though that absolved him of everything. And yet he wanted to be taken seriously too. This wanting it both ways is a common disease in Dutch intellectual discourse, exemplified by some of the writers Van Gogh admired most. Its destructive power can be cushioned in a narrow society where everyone knows the rules of the game. When it is exposed to outsiders with a less playful view of words, the effects can be devastating.

4.

We sat on the sidewalk terrace of a coffeeshop in The Hague, not far from the medieval Dutch parliament, barricaded against terrorist attacks with bollards. Farhane, a short, baby-faced man in his early twenties, gave the thumbs-up sign to various passersby. A few even merited a high five. This was his town, he told me, people knew him here. He was a real "Hague kid." His soft, cherubic features offered a peculiar contrast to his chest and arms, which were those of a trained fighter—he was keen on tac kwon do, the Korean martial art. We talked about theater, about Van Gogh and his murder, about 9/11, and about what it was like to grow up Moroccan-Dutch in The Hague.

Farhane's family is in fact unusually successful. His father taught himself to speak Dutch and owned several shops in The Hague. His two elder brothers were the first Moroccans to finish the prestigious Gymnasium Haganum. One works as an IT expert for the ministry of justice, the other for a large insurance firm. "I was the exception," Farhane said. "Everything was fine until I screwed up."

Farhane quit school, joined a gang, got involved in various crimes, was sent to a juvenile detention center, and ended up in a school for difficult children, where he learned nothing. Kids just sat around reading comics and smoking dope. One girl committed suicide on the third day he was there. He decided that this was no place to linger and robbed the headmaster in order to get expelled: "If I hadn't robbed him, I'd still be sitting there, smoking dope, reading comics, and getting into fights."

One of Farhane's earliest and bitterest memories goes back to when he was six. It still fills him with anger. The parents of his best friend, a Dutch kid, wouldn't let them play together. He wasn't even invited to his friend's birthday party. It was clear that he was not wanted. "That's something you never forget. Even though I wasn't so aware of what it meant at the time, it haunted me when I was a teenager. The worst thing is to be put in a box, to be told you don't belong. So you join others who're in the same box."

In Morocco, he explained, children play in the streets, but they're never out of sight. Everyone knows each other. Adults look out for other people's kids. But life in The Hague is different. The boys are let loose, as if they were in a Moroccan village, but no one keeps an eye on them. They run wild because there is nobody to tell them what's right or wrong. The parents themselves don't know how to cope with practical things, so their children have to help them with everything, filling out forms, and the like. That's why children lose trust in their own parents. You end up feeling angry.

With your parents? "No, with the Dutch state, which let us come here without explaining how things work. They let our parents clean the streets, work in factories, fix everything, but it's up to us, the children, to solve their problems. We can't blame our parents. We just can't rely on them."

I thought of another Dutchman of Moroccan descent whom I had met not long before, in Rotterdam, where he worked for a famous architectural firm. His father had also come to Holland as a guest worker, but had never owned anything himself. Although not an uneducated man—he went to a Koranic school in Morocco—he worked at a menial job in the same furniture factory for twenty-five years. Samir, the son, was born in Morocco, but joined his father when he was three. He remembers seeing his father at work, and noticed how his colleagues made jokes at his expense. There was no malice in what they said, just condescension. They treated his father as if he were a child. "That hurt," he said. "It's like seeing your mother being scolded by some Dutch woman in a store for not speaking Dutch properly."

He felt embarrassed for his parents, not because they didn't see what was going on, but because they had to pretend not to. They were too proud to show their humiliation, and so their children felt it all the more. When his father had worked at the factory for twenty-five years, he was picked up, as a special treat, to go to work in the boss's car. That was all. "That's when I saw how much respect he was given."

Did his father ever regret having come to the Netherlands? "No, he didn't, because he sacrificed everything for us to have a better life. He wanted me to become a doctor, the safest option. He doesn't understand why I wanted to become an architect. He thinks I'm a kind of bricklayer."

Farhane speaks Dutch to his brothers. With his parents he speaks Berber as well as Dutch. "About fifty-fifty," he said. Samir, the architect, said he still felt "like a guest in this country." I asked Farhane whether he ever felt Dutch. "Neither Dutch, nor Moroccan," he replied. What if Holland plays soccer against Morocco? "Then I'm for Morocco, for sure! But if I had to choose between a Dutch passport and a Moroccan one, I would choose the Netherlands. You have to think of your interests. A Moroccan passport would be useless. But with soccer I can choose for my own blood."

The day Theo van Gogh died, Farhane was on a train bound for Amsterdam. He was going to meet a writer to discuss a film script, and he knew something was up because people had called him on his mobile phone. By a bizarre coincidence, the writer lived on the street where Van Gogh was murdered. When Farhane arrived at his house, Van Gogh's corpse was still lying on the bicycle path under a blue plastic sheet. Farhane, like many Moroccan-looking people that day, was pursued by reporters who wanted to get his reaction. He refused to talk. "Those journalists had no respect," he said.

Farhane owed a lot to Van Gogh. Without him, he would never have become an actor. He enjoyed working with him. Theo was always open to discussion. But now he had to explain to other Moroccans that *Cool!* had been made before *Submission,* the film Van Gogh made with Ayaan Hirsi Ali, for otherwise he "would have been seen as a traitor."

He had seen only a small bit of the eleven-minute film. "It was totally ridiculous, totally missing the point." Van Gogh must have been "tricked into making such a film." Projecting the Koran onto the naked body of a woman is "an insult, the kind of insult I could never forget, like that time I wasn't allowed to play with my best friend at school. All Moroccans feel that way. I would never support Mohammed Bouyeri. But about the film he was right."

Right to kill Van Gogh? Farhane frowned, and played with his empty Coca-Cola glass. He found it easier not to speak entirely for himself: "No Moroccan respects Mohammed Bouyeri. To commit a murder during Ramadan—that is totally unacceptable." It was an odd answer that I had not expected. What did the fasting season have to do with the right to commit murder? Farhane looked pensive, then said: "Well, murder is never justified. Mohammed was not acting alone, of course. He was just a crazy guy. Mad! But I can see how one can be pushed into it."

Farhane saw how extremists began to emerge after 9/11. He still meets them from time to time in coffeehouses around The Hague. They say things there which they would never say in front of a camera. Only the other day someone said millions of Muslim women wanted to marry Mohammed Bouyeri. "You get pushed into it," Farhane repeated. "Just like me, you get into the wrong crowd of people, who are in the same boat as you, whose values are different from those in Holland. It doesn't happen overnight. Like dope, it is a gradual thing: you start off with a toke, then a few more puffs. Then you roll a joint . . ."

5.

It's not in Amsterdam that the demographic change in Holland is most visible. Though not quite a metropolis, Amsterdam is still a city where people are used to seeing foreigners. Even in Rembrandt's day there were large communities of strangers. More startling is the change in small provincial towns, where nothing much has happened since the war against Spain almost five hundred years ago. I knew Amersfoort, near Utrecht, only as the place where my grandparents moved into a retirement home. This is not a fair perspective, to be sure, but Amersfoort, with its pretty fifteenth-century church spire, its medieval market square, and its pleasant suburban houses, seemed like a place of deep provincial torpor, comfortable and very dull. Mondrian was born there, but left when he was eight. The only other thing of note is that the woods on the edge of town were the site of one of the most vicious Nazi concentration camps: *Polizeiliches Durchgangslager Amersfoort.*

Of the 129,720 citizens of Amersfoort, almost 21 percent are now of foreign origin. The police estimate that 40 percent of the Moroccan boys between the ages of fifteen and seventeen are suspected of criminal behavior. It is a vague statistic. What does "suspected" mean? This may simply be a reflection of local prejudices, or perhaps the situation is worse than the figures suggest. It is impossible to know for sure.

In the shadow of the Church Tower of Our Lady, I had tea with Bellari Said, a small, trim man, born in Morocco, who spoke Dutch with the strong southern lilt of Limburg, near the Belgian border. It is an accent that normally can mean only one thing to a Dutch person: that the speaker's family is Catholic. This is no longer the case, of course. Bellari Said was a Limburger too. As we spoke, young men and women on stilts, dressed in grotesque animal masks and strange peaked hats, were moving across the market square, frightening the children, perhaps reenacting some medieval pageant.

Bellari is another Moroccan success story. His parents are illiterate villagers from the Rif. Yet he has two university degrees, is active in politics, and practices psychiatry. Bellari's politics are a mixture of leftist Third Worldism, with a particular animus against Israel and the United States, and an active interest in the Muslim identity. Hence his membership in Abou Jahjah's European-Arab League and his desire to start a Muslim political party in the Netherlands. Since 9/11 and the murder of Van Gogh, Bellari is worried about the rule of law. Never in thirty years had he "seen a similar threat to the constitutional state."

Despite his feelings about Israel—"the West will only be reconciled with the Islamic world once Israel ceases to exist"—he sees the powerful "Jewish lobby" in the United States as an example for European Muslims. There should be an Islamic lobby of that kind in Europe, and Islamic schools, a recognized Islamic university, Islamic hospitals, and so forth. Only then can the new Europeans take their rightful places as citizens. The notion of secularizing Islam, in his view, is nonsense; it simply won't happen. Instead, religion must be used to harness Muslims to the constitutional state.

I was less interested in Bellari's politics than in his work as a psychiatrist. He had some specific data about immigrants that were, to say the least, arresting. The main problems among his patients, he said, were depression and schizophrenia: depression was especially common among women, and schizophrenia among men. But schizophrenia did not seem to affect first-generation immigrants. The guest workers tended to become depressed, not schizophrenic. It was the second generation of Moroccans, born and educated in the Netherlands, that suffered from schizophrenia. A young Moroccan male of the second generation was ten times more likely to be schizophrenic than a native Dutchman from a similar economic background.

There are several possible explanations for these startling figures. A sense of humiliation could be a factor, or the fact that immigrants tend to visit a psychiatrist only when things have come to a crisis. But Bellari has a theory about schizophrenia. He believes that the problem lies in the adaptation of a strictly regulated society to a freer, more open one. This can lead to disintegration of the personality. The pressure to assimilate is one of the risk factors for schizophrenia. Men suffer more than women because they have more freedom to interact with mainstream Western society. When the process of integration goes too fast, when the son of Moroccan villagers throws himself too quickly into the bewildering maelstrom of Western temptations, his "cognitive wiring" can go badly awry. The desire for strict religious rules is a form of nostalgia, as it were, a way to regain the world of one's parents, or what people think was the world of their parents. To remain sane, they long for the security of a paradise lost.

Girls, or young women, have the opposite problem. They have to live with many traditional constraints; the old order still exists for many of them, and so they long for more freedom. Bellari is a sophisticated man, and he worries about the consequences of religious extremism. But he, like most Muslims I talked to, had little sympathy for Ayaan Hirsi Ali. He thinks she has gone too far. "Look at her," he says. "She's a typical example of what I'm talking about. Having fought for her freedom, she goes berserk whenever she sees anything that smacks of the old ways that she grew up with."

Too much freedom, then, would seem to be a bad thing. Muslims of the second or even third generation need religion "as a stabilizing factor. It will help people integrate better, make them more altruistic, keep them on the right path." It is a strangely conservative view for a man who thinks of himself as a leftist. He is convinced that only properly organized religion will stop young men from downloading extremism from the Internet.

The yearning for the safe strictures of tradition also explains, in his opinion, why Muslim men prefer to marry girls from Morocco. Muslim girls born in the Netherlands are too threatening. And that is why, according to Bellari, more and more Muslim girls will end up marrying non-Muslims.

He may be right, even though this doesn't match the general impression that people have of Muslim women in the Netherlands. Perhaps because women in headscarves and veils, let alone burqas, are more conspicuous, it is women, more than men, who are the walking symbols of the kind of alien fundamentalism that many people fear. Yet the impression one gets of young Muslim women just from strolling around a Dutch city center is mixed and inconclusive: girls in headscarves and long dresses walk arm in arm with others in tank tops and jeans. It is as though religious attire is often worn as a fashion statement, or an assertion of difference, as much as a sign of devotion.

6.

Few people in Holland remember how recently emancipation of women came to the Dutch, or to other Europeans for that matter. In 1937, the Catholic minister for social affairs, C. P. M. Romme, wanted to prohibit all married women from working. Until 1954, women in government jobs were automatically fired when they got married. These were thought to be necessary measures to protect family life. Change came around the same time that Christian churches began to lose their grip. Perhaps because these shifts are still within living memory, another shift occurred more recently, among "progressives"—from a position of automatic, almost dogmatic advocacy of multicultural tolerance to an anxious rejection of Islam in public life.

I was told a fascinating story by a friend of mine named Jolande Withuis, a historian, writer, and well-known feminist with impeccable left-wing credentials. Her father was for many years an editor of the Communist Party newspaper. She told me her story over lunch in Amsterdam, when we talked about the response to Islamist terrorism, which she described as rather mild compared to the way Communists were harassed in the past. She recalled how Dutch Communists were persecuted after Soviet tanks crushed the Hungarian uprising in 1956. "Compared to how they suffered," she said, "Muslims are treated very gently."

When I pointed out that Islam, as a highly diverse religion with no central organization, could not really be compared to parties that took their orders straight from Moscow, she agreed, but still believed that there was a fundamental problem with Islam. She then told me a personal story about a well-known liberal doctor in Amsterdam who had fired his assistant for refusing to take off her headscarf at work.

This was seen by many people at the time as an intolerant act, unbecoming a liberal living in a multicultural society. But Jolande defended the doctor. The relationship with a doctor, she argued, especially for a female patient, is a very intimate one based on trust. When a medical assistant refuses to remove her scarf, trust is undermined, because it implies that women who reveal their hair are immoral. That is why women should not be allowed to wear a headscarf in any public capacity, not as a doctor's assistant, certainly not as a judge, and not in schools either.

I wondered about this. Muslim headscarves are worn for a variety of reasons, and do not necessarily imply disapproval of women who don't. As long as the medical assistant's faith did not impinge on her professional duties, the scarf should not be a problem. If, for example, she were unable to deal with male bodies, that would be a problem. Otherwise, why not treat the scarf as a personal matter, like a cross or Star of David worn around the neck?

We continued our discussion in e-mails. Meanwhile, I had met another former leftist who had turned against the multicultural faith: Paul Scheffer, who wrote the famous, and to some people notorious, essay "The Multicultural Drama," in which he had argued that the benign neglect of Muslim immigration by Dutch politicians was turning into a disaster. Like Jolande Withuis, he too saw Islam as a problem. Allowing large communities of alienated Muslims to grow in our midst was a recipe for social and political catastrophe.

I did not know Scheffer personally when we met at his house in south Amsterdam. It was a large house on a pleasant, leafy street, a mere five minutes' walk from a famous street market where Moroccans, Turks, Asians, Surinamese, and people from many other parts of the world plied their wares, surrounded by the sights and sounds and smells of a multicultural casbah: couscous, fresh red peppers, spicy sausages, vats of yogurt and cucumber, humus and tabouleh, tropical fish, mangoes and great spiky durians. Egyptian pop songs, Hindu film tunes, and Surinamese rap were blasted from CD and DVD stores. A slogan daubed in white paint on a red brick wall advocated the freedom of the Kurdish people.

Scheffer, with his jeans, wild curly hair, and casual shirt, looked every inch the progressive Dutch journalist, the kind who would have been a Provo in the 1960s. Once a Communist, he has had a serious impact on liberal public opinion with his writings on immigration. We met in his comfortable study, surrounded by books. After pouring me a glass of white wine, he sat back in his chair and gave me his views. Social life, he said, echoing Jolande's story about the doctor, has to be based on a certain degree of trust, on being on the same wavelength. When you have too many people whose cultures and values are utterly different from your own, that trust can no longer be sustained. Even with his closest Muslim friends, he said, he felt that he could never be sure they had the same understanding, the same references, the same sense of humor. It was wrong of past Dutch governments to hand citizenship to foreigners without giving any thought to the consequences. He told me how on one occasion he had stood in line at the international airport in Istanbul, and of the ten Dutch citizens in front of him, none spoke Dutch. "That," he said, "was when I felt a deep sense of betrayal."

One of the admirable things about Scheffer is his political enthusiasm. He isn't just a talker. He feels so strongly about the Dutch crisis that he wants to go into politics, perhaps even lead the Social Democratic Party. I mentioned the fact that Michael Ignatieff, the well-known Canadian writer and scholar, was planning to do something similar in Canada. "Right," said Scheffer, "you see, that's what I mean: you and I meet for the first time, yet you mention Ignatieff as though I've naturally heard of him. You are right, of course. I *have* heard of him. That's because we share the same culture. We can assume a common understanding."

I didn't say so at the time, but I couldn't help thinking that Michael Ignatieff's name would mean as little to most Dutch natives as to the bearded Moroccans in the nearby street market. I sensed a certain nostalgia in Scheffer's talk, a longing for an earlier age when the young intellectuals of Amsterdam felt like world pioneers in a new age of sexual and religious liberation, pioneers who shared the same ideas, the same values, the same references. The Muslims are the spoilsports, unwelcome crashers at the party. Scheffer's politics are not the same as Pim Fortuyn's. Yet the two share a certain yearning for something that may never really have existed, but whose loss is felt keenly nonetheless.

When I mentioned to Jolande Withuis the name of a conservative Dutch academic who believes we should combat Islamic intolerance by returning to the spirit of the classics, the values of ancient Athens, she was quick to reject that notion. She certainly didn't share the fond feelings many conservatives have for the 1950s either, although "the country was certainly less full and less violent then." No, her concern was for "the precarious gains of gender equality and gay rights. I find it terrible that we should be offering social welfare or subsidies to people who refuse to shake hands with a woman."

Tolerance, then, has its limits even for Dutch progressives. It is easy to be tolerant of those who are much like ourselves, whom we feel we can trust instinctively, whose jokes we understand, who share our sense of irony and might even have heard of Michael Ignatieff. It is much harder to extend the same principle to strangers in our midst, who find our ways as disturbing as we do theirs, who watch fearfully as their own children, caught in between, slip from the paternal grasp into a new and bewildering world. Jolande Withuis and Paul Scheffer, like Theo van Gogh, are quite ready to extend their hands to those children, so long as they renounce the same things that Dutch progressives renounced not so very long ago. But this will not help those who go the other way and seek salvation, or at least a degree of comfort, in the reinvention of tradition.

7.

M.L., a young woman born in Morocco, was dressed in a blue T-shirt and jeans, the summer uniform of most Dutch women in their twenties. She joined her father in the Netherlands when she was six, and was raised in The Hague. I had been given M.L.'s e-mail address by Jolande. M.L. worked in a home for battered women, mostly immigrants. She had also made a documentary film, together with three other Moroccan-Dutch women, all in their twenties, about violence against women. Inspired by Samira Bellil's autobiographical book, *In the Hell of the Tournantes,* about being gang-raped by Arab men in a Parisian ghetto, M.L. and her friends traveled to Paris to talk to activists for female rights. One reason Bellil, the daughter of Algerian immigrants, and other young women like her, got treated like whores, or worse, was their refusal to wear headscarves or veils—their preference, in other words, to look like other European women of their age.

I asked M.L. and her friend and colleague B.F. what they thought of the headscarf issue. M.L. talked about her old neighborhood in The Hague, an area I remember from my childhood as dank and gray, a place that combined the cramped quarters of the inner city with the lifelessness of a suburb. The streets are now, in M.L.'s phrase, "dominated by headscarves." For that reason alone, she doesn't much like hanging out there. But when I cited the opinion of Jolande and Ayaan Hirsi Ali, among others, that headscarves are a symbol of female oppression, M.L. cried: "Bullshit!"

She continued: "Women who don't wear headscarves are also fucking oppressed—perhaps more so than those who do. What's the fucking problem? Those headscarves? My sisters wear them, but they don't give a shit that I don't. It means nothing, that headscarf."

M.L. had a tendency to sound more sure of herself than she really was. She would quickly qualify her statements with doubts. On the link between Islam and violence against women, for example, she differed with her friend, B.F., who blamed Islam. M.L. thought it had more to do with Moroccan village culture, where "it's normal for women to be beaten."

This is a question that comes up again and again. After showing their documentary film in Amsterdam, M.L. and her friends encouraged people to "break the taboos" and have a public debate on the abuse of women. A Moroccan-Dutch woman named Loubna Berrada told the audience that "culture and religion are used to justify violence. If a girl calls herself a victim, she is blamed. If she goes to the police or social workers, she is a traitor. All my Turkish and Moroccan girlfriends have had to cope with domestic violence."

This statement from a woman who had suffered herself was met with agreement as well as anger. "It's good that you came here," said a girl in the audience, "but leave our culture out of it. Then nobody will see you as a traitor."[2] Many people applauded her for this. The defense of one's culture or religion is understandable in a hostile environment, but it's hard to see how these issues can be discussed without reference to culture.

M.L.'s father, like most fathers who came to find work in the Netherlands, is religious in a customary way. That is, he tries to stick to the traditions of his native place without making a fetish of them, or even giving them much thought. When M.L. is home and her father comes back from the mosque, she asks him "what nonsense the imam was talking this time." The answer usually comes in a comment about his daughter's habits. It's always about the daughter, said M.L., "the daughter, the daughter, the daughter—how we dress too provocatively, blah blah blah."

Her mother, on the other hand, is more reflective. She began studying religion and consequently, in M.L.'s words, "became a fanatic." She wants M.L. to wear a headscarf. "She knows how to play on my guilt. My father only cares about forms, about what the outside world will think. For the rest, he's cool. But my mother is different. I have one sister and six brothers. We all rebelled against our parents. My mother thinks she's being punished by God. . . . We were raised with the idea that everything is forbidden, that you go to hell if you do this or that. Of course, you do these things anyway, secretly, but I'm still frightened of those punishments. You're not allowed to have any doubts about faith. When I tell my mother about my doubts, she goes crazy." B.F., who had been listening to this with a knowing smile, added in her thick Amsterdam accent: "My mother taught us a lot that has nothing to do with Islam—those old village ways that have nothing to do with me."

Yet even B.F. said she felt guilty: "When I make love to my boyfriend, I get into a panic. But it feels so good that you still do it, even though it's forbidden by God." M.L. giggled: "The most important thing is virginity. We carry the family honor. I was terrified of getting pregnant, even after just kissing a guy." Both women collapsed in laughter, slapping hands. M.L. remembered wearing her brother's jeans one day, and when her period was late, she thought that maybe the jeans had made her pregnant. "You know," said M.L., suddenly looking serious, "you think you're living the way you want. But actually, without realizing it, you're still living the way your mother wants."

After going to a "black" high school that was composed

almost entirely of immigrant children, M.L. took a course at a hotel school. It was her first confrontation with native Dutch kids. "I felt so free! Suddenly I could talk about anything. This gives you the illusion that Holland is perfect. Your expectations are so high that you can be easily disappointed. I think I have a more balanced perspective now. But I still don't always know what the hell I'm doing. It's so hard to make choices. To do what you have to do, you have to be at war with your parents."

Since their parents couldn't tell them how to live in a European society, the girls had to find other channels of instruction. "This might sound stupid," M.L. said, "but I learned how to behave, how to talk to people, from television. Even sexual things we learned from TV. At home we never talked about such things. The biggest barrier to integration is not Dutch society; it's our parents."

One of M.L.'s brothers has a native Dutch girlfriend, with whom he had a child. They live together. This was not easy for his mother to accept. But now she dotes on the baby. Her brother is unusual, M.L. explained. Mostly, she said, Moroccan guys take Dutch girlfriends for sex, because Dutch girls are easy, but then marry a girl from Morocco. "Mountain goats" was M.L.'s phrase for these imported village girls. Most of the battered women in the shelter where she works are "mountain goats." Moroccan guys, she said, prefer them because they want to marry virgins, who'll do as they're told. Moroccan guys, she said, are "fucking unreliable."

8.

M.L. and B.F. might be exceptional cases, but I'm not sure that they are. They may in fact be articulating very common experiences, and headscarves are not a reliable guide to what young women are thinking. Some wear them just to please their parents, and take them off whenever the parents are out of sight. Others wear them as protection against harassment from Muslim men. And some wear them because their faith gives them comfort. Perhaps the most impressive young woman I ran across during my time in Holland was Nora Choua, a law student at Nijmegen University and the head of the Union of Islamic Students. Nora wore a black chador that left only her round, friendly face, with a touch of lipstick and mascara, open to the eyes of the world.

Nijmegen, where Nora was born, is a small town on the border of Germany rich in European history. Traditionally a Catholic town, it was also an ancient Roman settlement. Drusus used it as an army camp for his expeditions against the German tribes. Charlemagne once resided in Nijmegen. And Frederick Barbarossa built a castle on the site of Charlemagne's palace. A chapel is all that remains of Barbarossa's castle, overlooking the River Waal, whose bridge was captured by Allied paratroopers in 1944, before they embarked on their fatal attempt to take Arnhem.

My grandfather was posted in Nijmegen after World War I as a minister for the small and highly liberal Mennonite community.

My father attended the public Gymnasium in the 1930s. It was a secular oasis in this largely Catholic town, where Protestants and Jews, as well as a smattering of Catholics from the upper middle class, shared the same classrooms. Walking around Nijmegen one Saturday afternoon with my father, we found the old Gymnasium exactly as it had been when he was a pupil, the bronze school name still embedded in the red brick wall above the elegant art deco entrance. A number of disheveled men stood around talking. When we stepped inside to take a look, a black man with bloodshot eyes waved us back. "You can't go in," he said. Why not? "Don't you know?" he said. "This is a Catholic center for drug addicts."

And so we walked back toward the town center, a pleasant hodgepodge of nineteenth-century storefronts and a few sixteenth- and seventeenth-century buildings, blighted by developments from the 1960s. It was market day. I heard a lot of Dutch spoken in the unmistakable accent of the south, as well as Turkish, Arabic, Cantonese, and Berber.

Nora and I met at a café on the Waal within sight of the bridge that the Allies took from the Germans. She told me about her family. Both her brothers were living with Dutch girls, which is a problem because the girls can't really communicate with her parents. But Nora has no problem visiting them. She doesn't condemn her brothers, or her sister, who doesn't wear a veil, and once even dyed her hair blond.

It was the usual story: Nora's father left Morocco and came to Holland in 1963, after working in Spain, France, and Belgium. He took the hardest factory jobs, often working the night shifts. Although he had wanted to learn to speak Dutch properly, his boss dissuaded him. Unnecessary for his line of work, he said. Now he is semi-retired, suffering from hernias, diabetes, and a stomach disease. Nora's mother is more religious than her husband, but with a lot of common sense. There is not a lot of talk about burning in hell in Nora's family. But when Nora wanted to study law, her parents had little idea what that meant. The law was not a familiar concept, at least not as something one would study.

Nora's interest in law began early. In high school, she was always joining in class debates. She had "a big mouth." It was then that she learned about the Dutch constitution. It gave her "such a wonderful feeling. The idea that everyone is equal, the freedom of religion." Now, her feeling is less positive. She feels that freedom of speech is being stretched too far. At a recent student debate on terrorism, a law student claimed to be proud of the constitution, because it allowed Theo van Gogh to speak his mind. That, said Nora, was "hypocritical." She thought that he only said it because Van Gogh's insults didn't offend *him*. Because he agreed with Van Gogh's views. But why should anyone have the right to insult others on the grounds of race or creed? Nora pointed out that this was against the law.

Nora was still in high school when the Twin Towers came down in New York. Everything changed on that day, for her and in how she was seen in the eyes of others. "Before, I was just Nora. Then, all of a sudden, I was a Muslim." She recalled how she was a little late for class on the eleventh of September. When she entered the classroom, everyone turned to look at her, expecting her to say something, perhaps even make some statement, since she normally had such a big mouth. But she was "speechless." She felt that all Muslims were being blamed, especially after the same frightening images were shown over and over on the television news, not only of the smoking towers in Manhattan, but of young Muslims dancing with joy in a small Dutch town called Ede.

September 11 had made Muslims think about things more seriously than before. What things? "Things like: What right does Osama bin Laden have to call himself a Muslim. Or things like the correct understanding of jihad." Jihad, she said, did not give her "a bad feeling." People often don't understand it: "Young Moroccan boys shout about jihad, but that's just macho talk. They have little idea what it means. Jihad is only justified in self-defense, if you're attacked, or if you cannot practice your faith."

Faith, however, remains a private affair for Nora. She is not in favor of introducing Shariah, or Islamic, law into Dutch legislation, "because it doesn't fit in this country, and besides, I'm for the separation of church and state." She would never even think of living in a country like Saudi Arabia, where women can't get a driver's license, or Nigeria, where adulterous women are stoned. Nora is not interested in a Muslim political party either, for "the Dutch population is varied and the government must take that into account." She is, in fact, a member of the Young Socialists, part of the PVDA.

Nora is a devout Muslim, then, who can see the point of jihad in defense of her faith, but also a progressive Dutch citizen full of common sense, whose talents and ambition should be of benefit to society. But she knows things are not that simple. For if 9/11 provoked a shift in the attitudes of Dutch progressives, things changed for the immigrants as well. Nora describes it as a "switch." Before 9/11, well-educated Moroccans had confidence in their future in Dutch society. This is where they felt they belonged. It was the un-educated who felt isolated, or indifferent. They still are indifferent, according to Nora. But the educated ones have changed. They have become frightened to be identified as Muslims or Moroccans. Yet it is precisely those people who should be given every chance, those young people who have tried so hard to succeed. For when they are disappointed, when they see the door being slammed in their faces, they become embittered.

"I would hate for that to happen to me," said Nora, adjusting her scarf in the afternoon breeze coming from the river. She fell into a rare silence. I thought of frustrated intellectuals, not just Muslims or Moroccans, and their vulnerability to great revolutionary causes when they feel marginalized or cornered. I thought of Farhane, the actor, and his bitterness about being ostracized and "put in a box."

I asked Nora what she would like to do after she got her university degree. She didn't want to work as a barrister, she said. She didn't think the law court was the right place for a woman in a headscarf, for counsel and judges had to look neutral. She would prefer a government job. "But, you know . . . ," she said, "it is so sad that you cannot work for the city government if you wear a Jewish kippa or a Muslim headscarf. After all, this city belongs to me too. It's as if you are mentally disappeared." It was a strange and haunting phrase, "mentally disappeared," something worse than being ignored or treated with indifference. It is as if by a mental effort society pretends that you don't even exist.

The sense of being "disappeared" can lead to aggression, as well as self-hatred; dreams of omnipotence blend with the desire for self-destruction. To prove their existence, to themselves and the world, people sometimes join great revolutionary causes, or embark on a mission to spread the word of God. Others, even more desperate, might commit a spectacular crime, like vengeful gods, assassinating a famous person, or shooting at random into a terrified crowd. Some lost souls, in order to feel truly alive, to prove their individuality, have to kill it in the process: suicide as the ultimate act of will. These are the most dangerous "radical losers," the lone killers who cannot bear to live with themselves any longer and want to drag the world down with them.*

---

*The phrase "radical losers" was coined by Hans Magnus Enzensberger in a brilliant essay in *Der Spiegel*, November 2005.

FIVE

Submission

Fuck Hirsi Ali Somali
Just two months in Holland, and already so knowing
Cancer whore, shit stain, I'll smash your face . . .

Et cetera. This is only the beginning of a rap number by a three-man hip-hop band named DHC, living in The Hague ("The Hague is my terrain"). The lyrics, originally written in Dutch, get more graphic ("I cut you up in two"). Imagery of the circumcision Ayaan Hirsi Ali suffered as a child is repeated as a ghastly refrain. The rap was supposedly meant for the group's private pleasure, but quickly got spread around the Internet, was picked up by a television news program, and became a scandal. Hirsi Ali sued. The band was arrested, tried, convicted, and sentenced to 150 hours of community work. The three men are of Moroccan origin.

No one who has seen or heard Ayaan Hirsi Ali can be indifferent to her. To some she is a heroine, standing up against the forces of darkness, battling for free speech and enlightened values. Men are charmed by her extraordinary beauty. Her slender, dark elegance and shy smile give her a chic vulnerability that looks very fine on the cover of magazines. Theo van Gogh's typical response, after his first meeting with her, was that he'd "love to fuck her."[1] Which may be why women sometimes distrust her. Others, women and men, actively loathe her. This loathing is harder to place. The haters are sometimes old progressives, who see her as a right-wing troublemaker in the multicultural garden. Some hate her for being a black woman who became too prominent—an alien who needed to be cut down to size. More often the haters are fellow immigrants, usually Muslims. Hirsi Ali's hostile views on Islam would account for this, but there is something else, a deeper resentment, revealed in the rap number, which is both oddly Dutch and also typical of a particular kind of immigrant's rage. Hirsi Ali doesn't act "normal." She puts on airs after "just two months in Holland." She "prances around" like an *autochtoon* (native-born person).

A Dutch hip-hop label owner said in defense of the rappers that Ayaan Hirsi Ali "has offended many people deeply with her statements. Why should she be able to get away with that, just because she studied and learned to neatly package her statements, whereas DHC cannot, because they are rough street kids who do so in their own language?"

In fact, Hirsi Ali never threatened anyone, but this argument illustrates the kind of resentment she provokes among many immigrants. The resentment goes something like this: She has studied, she can speak eloquently, even though she has only been in Holland for a short time. She thinks she's better than us, who were born here. Her statements are neatly packaged. She pretends to be Dutch, an indigenous clone.

DHC said they had never meant to hurt her physically. Their abuse was just words. If they had wanted to kill her, they said, they surely wouldn't have advertised their intentions. They were indeed words, and there is no proof that the three Moroccan-Dutch rappers in The Hague had anything more in mind than "dissing" their target. That's what rappers do; it's a style, just like the photograph of DHC, a gang of poseurs in jeans and face masks, pretending to be armed guerrillas. Rappers play at being murderers. Perhaps they were Dutch enough to have adopted the national penchant for vicious irony. But Mohammed Bouyeri did mean it when he pinned his death threat to Hirsi Ali onto Theo van Gogh's corpse. The difference between his words and those of DHC come down to one thing, which is not just a matter of style: to the rappers, she had betrayed her immigrant roots; to Mohammed, her betrayal was religious: she was an apostate.

2.

Ayaan Hirsi Ali's first act of serious rebellion took place in a cinema, in Kenya, where she lived with her family in exile for ten years. It was in the late 1980s, when the Iran-Iraq War was still raging and the fatwa was out against Salman Rushdie. Ayaan was a good Muslim—more than a good Muslim, in fact. Inspired by Sister Aziza, her favorite teacher at the Nairobi Muslim Girls' Secondary School, she covered herself from head to toe, demonstrated against Rushdie, and even considered fighting for the Iranian Islamic forces against Saddam Hussein's secular Iraq. She shocked her classmates by showing them pictures from jihadist magazines of murdered Muslims, and declared that she was ready to die for Allah. Contrary to Somali custom, she refused even to shake hands with a man.

But she also had a secret boyfriend, a Kenyan, who, though a devout Muslim, was ready to cut himself some slack. This was scandalous, not only because she was expected to produce sons with a member of her own clan; she was not allowed to have intimate relations with any boy. So they would meet in secret, in the dark, in the cinema. She can still remember the film they saw while they sat side by side, their hands touching. Just the feel of his hand made her break out in a sweat of guilty anxiety. Yet she couldn't contain herself. The film was *A Secret Admirer,* a Hollywood comedy of errors about the mixed-up love affairs of American high school kids. The fact that such a thing was possible, that young people kissed without fear, was a revelation.

On the screen was a vision of liberty, however zanily expressed, a vision associated with the West, with America, where her father, Hirsi Magan Isse, a political activist in opposition to the Somalian dictator Mohammed Siad Barre, had studied. A linguist by training, he believed in democracy, and in education for women, including his own daughters. The U.S. was his great example. If a young country like the U.S. could succeed, he told himself, then so could Somalia. He was in prison as a political dissident when Ayaan was born. They met for the first time when she was six. His name and his activities had reached Ayaan only through whispered conversations. Although estranged, she clearly still adores him.

Ayaan's rebellion was not against him—that would come later. He was mostly absent from Kenya anyway. Her immediate problem was sexual, but this had many implications: how to reconcile the teachings of Islam—the deepest beliefs of her mother and illiterate grandmother, of her favorite teacher, Sister Aziza, of her Kenyan boyfriend, herself, and even her progressive father—with her physical and emotional desires? Why could she and "Yussuf" (his secret name) only meet furtively, like thieves in the dark? Why did she have to lie all the time about something that felt so natural? What was it that separated her from the world of those American high school kids glimpsed on the cinema screen?

One of the most frequent criticisms made against Ayaan Hirsi Ali is her allegedly monolithic view of Islam. Like all major religions, the Muslim faith comes in many forms and degrees of orthodoxy. Some practices, such as female circumcision, are not religious, but cultural. In the case of Ayaan, it was the custom of her Somali clan, the Darod. While her father, an opponent of the custom, was abroad, her grandmother had Ayaan and her younger sister circumcised.

However, it is Ayaan's conviction that the social, economic, and political problems that plague the Islamic world—terrorism, poverty, dictatorship, lack of scientific progress—can be explained, at least in part, by something suffered by all Muslims, regardless of their culture, and that is a warped view of sexuality. It comes down to what Chafina, the young filmmaker in Amsterdam, said about her father and his imam: "Daughter, daughter, daughter"—the obsession with the family's honor resting on the purity of the women.

Ayaan Hirsi Ali writes about Muslim sexual morality that it "is derived from premodern tribal societies, but sanctified by the Koran and further developed in the stories about the life of the Prophet. For many Muslims this morality is expressed in the obsession with virginity. Such value is attributed to virginity that people are blinded to the human and social catastrophes that result from this obsession."[2]

Ayaan's grandmother kept a billy goat. In the evening, when the female goats belonging to the neighbor passed his patch, the goat would rush over and jump one of them. Shocked by this show of animal force, Ayaan asked her grandmother why the goat behaved so brutally. It's the fault of the neighbors, replied her grandmother. If they didn't want the females to be jumped, they should have taken a different path. To Ayaan, this anecdote serves as an illustration of what is wrong with Muslim morality. "As far as sex is concerned," she writes, "men are seen in Muslim culture as irresponsible, frightening beasts, who lose all self-control the moment they see a woman." This is not seen as the fault of men, but of the women who tempt them, simply by their physical presence. Hence the need for veils, for being kept out of sight.

Things seemed very different in the West. Ayaan could tell from the movie, and perhaps even from the English language itself. Somali was for storytelling, for myths and tribal lore; Arabic was the language of the Prophet. But English, to her, was the language of science, of reason. She needed English, the genteel, even somewhat prissy English of her Indian schoolteachers in Kenya, to "order my thoughts."

"The only real hope for Muslims," she wrote more than a decade after her experience in the Nairobi cinema, "is to practice self-criticism, to test those moral values, taken from the Koran. Only then can they hope to break out of the cage in which they imprison their women, and thereby themselves. The fifteen million Muslims who live in the West are in the most favourable circumstances to make this hope a reality."

In the West, she explained, Muslims can speak their minds without fear of punishment or death. Under such favorable circumstances, they would have to be almost perverse not to do so.

3.

Ayaan Hirsi Ali told me about her childhood one day as we drove through The Hague in a bulletproof car. She spoke softly, almost self-effacingly, but this was deceptive. For behind the polite smile and soft voice was a steeliness that deflected all challenges to her convictions. The head of her security detail was sitting in front. Another car drove ahead of us, scanning our route for potential trouble, and another followed behind. Ever since she began to speak out in Holland against the dangers of Muslim extremism, Ayaan has been followed by death threats. After her film *Submission* and the murder of Van Gogh, she has had to live virtually underground, first in military barracks and safe houses, then under permanent guard.

We passed through an area called Transvaal, near the soccer stadium, once a Dutch working-class neighborhood, now almost 100 percent *allochtoon,* an ugly, and relatively new, bureaucratic term for people of alien, but more specifically non-European, origin. Only a few days before, I had read a newspaper article about this area, which I used to cycle through as a child on the way to the stadium on Sunday afternoons. One of the few "native" inhabitants to have opted to stay was an old woman known as the Queen of Transvaal. She told her interviewer that the first foreigners to arrive were blacks from Suriname, in the 1960s. But they were okay.

"The trouble really began," she said, "when masses of Moroccan and Turkish families were dumped in our neighborhood. They had no idea how to behave in our society. Garbage bags would be tossed into the street from the second floor. Goats would be slaughtered on the balcony. That sort of thing. The worst, really, is that we don't speak the same language. You know, when your ceiling leaks and you can't tell the neighbors upstairs to turn off their tap. People get irritated."[3]

I thought of the Queen of Transvaal as we passed the neighborhood's dreary row houses, some with boarded-up windows and graffiti on the walls. Rubbish spilled on the sidewalks out of torn plastic bags. There was the usual profusion of satellite dishes. Most butchers in the main shopping street were halal. The coffeeshops and kebab joints certainly looked livelier than anything in the city of my childhood. But one cannot dismiss all the *autochtoon* people who moved out as racists. The Queen of Transvaal spoke a truth that those whose lives are insulated from the cultural frictions and general squalor of the "dish cities" prefer not to hear.

Ayaan Hirsi Ali hears it only too clearly. She has swept floors in factories, and interpreted for illiterate women who were paralyzed with fear and bewilderment in a society they could not even begin to understand. Some had been abused by husbands or fathers; others had contracted AIDS; yet others had lost their virginity and were married off to strangers. This was hardly the promised West that Hirsi Ali had dreamed of. As a politician, she has stood up for the Dutch "natives" who feel forced to abandon their homes to get away from the sacrificial goats, the imams who preach hatred of the West, the idle young men asking for trouble, and the neighbors who don't understand their language.

When we first met, in Paris, Ayaan said something few Dutch politicians would dare to utter. She was talking about policemen. The top officers, she said, were overpaid, ignorant, and lazy. The real hard work in a city like Amsterdam was done by underpaid cops in the streets, who did their best to deal with violence against women, drug traders, and religious tensions. But, she said, "these are the kind of people who are leaving the cities in droves. One day people will wake up and say: 'Oh my God, the whole city is black.' And what's happening in Amsterdam will happen in the whole country."

Ayaan's bodyguards in The Hague were dying to get out of "dish city." When Ayaan asked the man in the front seat whether we could stop the car, and maybe walk around a little, chat with the people, have a drink, he almost choked on his cold cup of coffee. "No way!" he said. "They'll recognize you instantly and then we'll have a serious problem. They'll spit on you, curse you. Let's get out of here quick!"

4.

Much of Ayaan's life has been spent on the run. Born in Somalia, in Mogadishu, she learned the politics of fear early on. These were "the whispering years," when her father was an absent rebel, and Ayaan and her sister and brother got punished at school for not singing songs in praise of

Mohammed Siad Barre, the dictator they had been taught at home to despise. When civil war broke out, the family fled to Saudi Arabia, where Ayaan saw her father for the first time, in Mecca. She never forgot her first impression of the new country: women dressed in black burqas, their eyes peering through tiny slits. The sinister influence of Wahhabism, the Saudi orthodoxy, had already made itself felt in Somalia too, through Saudi-trained imams. The loose, colorful garments of Somali tradition had begun to be replaced by black veils. But here everything was black.

Since the women were kept mostly at home, Ayaan and her sister watched a great deal of television. She recalls the bloody epics showing the Prophet's army crushing the barbarous world of wicked idolaters who were buried alive in the desert. She recalls the news programs of powerful men entertaining other powerful men, with not a woman in sight. When her brother was invited to accompany their father on hunting trips, she wondered why she wasn't allowed to take part. But she also remembers watching Egyptian soap operas that revealed glimpses of romance.

From Saudi Arabia, they were forced to move to Sudan, and then Ethiopia, to join other members of the Somali resistance. Ayaan's mother saw no point in sending her daughters to school, since they would soon be married off anyway. They were educated thanks only to their father's insistence. A year later, they moved again, to Kenya. Compared to Saudi

Arabia, or Ethiopia under Colonel Mengistu, Kenya was a paradise of liberty, although even there the shadow of imported Islamic orthodoxy was beginning to fall. Ayaan's younger sister, Haweya, always the more rebellious one, liked to wear short skirts, which her mother tore up in disgust. In her teens, Ayaan noticed how the girls in her school began to drop out. Some she saw a few years later, as tired housewives, worn down by their duty to produce sons.

And yet it was in Kenya that Ayaan was swept away herself by the wave of fundamentalism, which had begun in the Middle East and caught up with her in Africa. Sister Aziza, Ayaan's favorite teacher at the Muslim girls' school, was her prime inspiration, but she was also attracted to the ideas of the Muslim Brotherhood. Becoming a martyr, submitting to the will of Allah, wearing a black hijab over her school uniform, these were part of her teenage idealism. The other paradox of her early life is that she was saved from the fate of her classmates only by the departure of her father, who may have had liberal politics, but was a traditionalist in family matters. So was her mother, but she lacked the authority to impose her views. If her father had stayed, instead of leaving for Ethiopia in 1980 to live with another woman, Ayaan would have been forced into a marriage too, and become, in her phrase, "a factory of sons." Aged sixteen, there would have been no escape.

It happened instead when she was twenty-two, in 1992.

Her father decided that she was to marry a cousin in Canada. After a ceremony in Nairobi, where she met her husband-to-be for the first time, she boarded a flight to Germany, where she would stay with relatives before flying on to Canada. Her first sight of Europe was from the air, over Frankfurt. The landscape she recalls looked "so neat, so planned, so well ordered."

The uncle who was supposed to take care of her during the stopover in Germany would not let her stay. His German wife didn't want Somali relatives in the house. So she was passed on to an address in Bonn. After one night, she decided to bolt. "I had always told my father that I wanted to be independent. Now it was no longer theoretical. I had to take the plunge."

She had the telephone number of a Somali who worked at a center for asylum seekers in Holland. This person told her to contact a cousin in Volendam. With some trepidation, she boarded the train to Amsterdam and took a bus from there. It was an odd introduction to Dutch life. Volendam is a touristy fishing village where people still parade up and down in clogs, a picture postcard of traditional life, a kind of open-air museum. "All the pretty little houses were decorated in the same way," Ayaan remembers, "with lace curtains and flowers and plants. Everyone seemed to have the same taste." It was at once more oppressive than Kenya and much freer, a paradox that would continue to haunt her, even in her political career. The planning, the order, like that of the German landscape, the English language, the Dutch row houses, was admirable, yet the conformity and the rules were stifling.

There, amid the black caps and white bonnets, the clogs and the cheese farms, Ayaan was taken in by a Somali woman who had become an outcast in her family by marrying a Westerner. She advised Ayaan to seek political asylum, as forced marriage was not an acceptable ground for asylum. She should pretend to be fleeing from the civil war in Somalia. It was easy for Somalis to get refugee status. At the asylum center, Ayaan was even coached by a person from an NGO for refugees in how to answer questions. She changed her name and her date of birth, and said she had arrived from Mogadishu. A bogus asylum seeker, then? "Yes," said Ayaan, "a very bogus asylum seeker."

5.

Listening to Ayaan's story, I was reminded of another immigrant's story, that of the Iranian-born newspaper columnist and law professor in Leiden, Afshin Ellian. He had never been a radical Muslim. On the contrary, after the fall of the Shah, Ellian chose the losing side; he joined the leftist Tudeh Party, which was violently suppressed by the ruling clergy in the 1980s. Ellian was smuggled out of the country on the back of a camel and spent seven years in Kabul, where the Soviet-backed Communist regime allowed him to run a propaganda radio station. In Kabul he had to be protected against killer commandos from Iran. By 1989, he had broken with the leftists and had appealed to the UN for protection. With the help of the UN, he was invited to the Netherlands under a program for refugees, which in Ellian's words "pinned the label on me of an East European-style dissident." It is how he ended up in the Netherlands. His first impressions are worth recording.

Housed together with thirty Vietnamese in an elegant provincial hotel, the first thing he noticed was the "soft, peaceful greenness of Holland. So much peace and calm. It made me weep. When I saw people in the cafés and streets talking freely and laughing loudly, I lamented the fate of my old friends. For here, at last, was freedom. We had fought for it, but we had never actually seen it."

It is the typical vision of the type of person whom Arthur Koestler once described as the "internally bruised veteran of the totalitarian age." Koestler was referring to men such as himself, refugees from Hitler and Stalin, who regarded Britain as a kind of "Davos," a huge asylum with quiet green parks and naive people who never lived in fear, a wonderful resting place for the survivors of murderous regimes. Then and now, such veterans can appreciate like no others the blessings of freedom and peace, but cannot always hide their contempt for those who take it for granted.

If Ellian is angry at the Islamists, a greater fury is reserved for the West itself, a West that he, like Ayaan, has a tendency to idealize. This is not necessarily a paradox. Like many intellectuals from the non-Western world, Ellian is conscious of double standards. He is old enough to remember life under the Shah, backed by the United States. During the Iranian revolution, he recalls with a certain pride, "we showed how we could defy the most powerful nation on earth with empty hands. The West never gave us democracy. What was good enough for them should have been good enough for us."

Within a year of arriving in Holland, Ellian had learned fluent Dutch. In a little over five years, he had degrees in philosophy, international law, and criminal law. This feat of will and perseverance was less common in the Netherlands than in the U.S., which would have been Ellian's preferred destination. He set a standard that very few immigrants could meet. The question that haunted him, though, was not how to get on as an immigrant, or the problem of integration, but "why it was that Americans and Europeans managed to live together without cutting each other's throats—the question, that is, of liberty and the rule of law."

When on one occasion in 2005, Job Cohen, the mayor of Amsterdam, refused to use his riot police to crush a small

but noisy demonstration during a public memorial to the victims of slavery, as a result of which Rita Verdonk, the minister for integration, was unable to complete her speech,
Ellian pulled out all the stops. Amsterdam, he ranted, had
shown no tolerance for "dissidents." By dissidents he meant
people like Van Gogh, Ayaan Hirsi Ali, and himself. Amsterdam, he continued, had become a "free city for Muslim terrorists, left-wing extremists and organized crime. . . . After the
dissidents, it is now the turn of ministers to be barred from the
city. As long as the citizens of Amsterdam are unable to bring
about a political earthquake and get rid of the socialist mafia,
nothing will change." Shades here, perhaps, of the old radio
propagandist in Kabul.

Ayaan Hirsi Ali expresses herself more quietly, and with
a great deal more charm, but one can't help sensing that in
her battle for secularism, too, there are hints of zealousness,
echoes perhaps of her earlier enthusiasm for the Muslim
Brotherhood, before she was converted to the ideals of the
European Enlightenment.

6.

Our bulletproof convoy was approaching the area where
Ayaan spent her first years in the Netherlands. The
countryside was flat and green, the villages prosperous and

well maintained. We were in the heartland of strict Calvinism, deeply provincial, traditionally suspicious of outsiders, but with pockets of great wealth—large converted farmhouses and expensive villas. Ayaan's first home was a trailer in a refugee camp, in a forest near Lunteren, a village that was chosen by the Dutch Nazis as a site for mass rallies in the 1930s. A black boulder still marks the village as the precise center of the Netherlands. There, on sacred earth for Dutch blackshirts, the NSB pledged its loyalty to Nazi Germany in 1940.

But things have changed, even there in the rural center of Calvinism, fascism, and plush retirement homes. Lunteren belongs to Ede, a small town with some industry, mostly steel and technology. Several thousand Turkish and Moroccan workers settled there (fewer than ten live in lily-white Lunteren). Ede's dish city consists of charmless rows of four-story apartment blocks, only minutes away from the kind of neighborhood, with identical houses, identical lace curtains, and identical gardens, filled with identical garden gnomes, that struck Ayaan as both pretty and oppressive in Volendam. Laundry fluttered outside the windows, next to the satellite dishes. The streets were largely empty. It was there that a bunch of Muslim teenagers caused a national outrage by dancing with joy on the day the Twin Towers came down.

Much against the advice of her minders, Ayaan insisted on

taking a walk. "They will know it's you, and then there's bound to be trouble," said the chief minder. He was right about the first part. No sooner had we stepped out of the car than heads appeared at several windows hastily phoning friends and neighbors to spread the word of our presence. Security men in blazers looked nervously about, chattering on their phones. Whichever way the slim figure of Ayaan Hirsi Ali went, she was shadowed by her entourage of bodyguards, a spectacle that no doubt attracted far more attention than if she had been there alone.

Ayaan had really wanted to go to England, but the longer she stayed in Holland, the more she wished to make her life there. Her aim was to learn the language as quickly as she could and study politics. Like Ellian, she wanted to unravel the mystery of a society at peace. Coming from a continent of almost perpetual violence, she wanted to know how a people could live freely without murdering one another. But first she had to fight against the strictures of Dutch bureaucracy. Instead of allowing her to take Dutch language classes, they wanted to get her jobs for which she was unsuited, jobs that required no language ability but a large tolerance for boredom. The government would pay for vocational training so she could be some kind of clerk. She felt that welfare agencies and social workers were stifling her ambition.

For a while, she lived near the dish city in Ede with another Somali woman and worked in a factory. But this was not getting her anywhere either. So she advertised for a Dutch language teacher at a local church. Her request was answered by a married couple, high school teachers, who eventually took her into their home, where she learned not only the language, but the manners, customs, habits, and traditions of the Dutch middle class. Theirs was an orderly household, a microcosm of the country Ayaan had first encountered, both much stuffier and much freer than Kenya, its egalitarianism and individual liberties bound to strict, even rigid rules. Family dinners started promptly at six, appointments had to be kept precisely on time, household chores had to be equally shared.

It was a slow and rocky process, and assimilation was far from complete. But Ayaan did learn to speak perfect Dutch. She still calls her teacher, a friendly woman in her late forties, "my Dutch mother." After the minders had checked the area for safety, we dropped by for a cup of coffee. It was a neat and orderly house, with nothing casual or slapdash about it. Everything had its place. A sponge cake was cut into perfect little slices, and the coffee was brewed just right. Both husband and wife made it clear to me that they didn't wish to be identified, for they were "afraid of reprisals, especially after the death of Theo van Gogh." Did they really think they were in any danger just because they had taught

Ayaan Hirsi Ali to speak Dutch? "I'm angry about this my-self," replied the husband, a trim man with close-cropped hair and light blue eyes, "but that's the way it is. There are many Moroccans in Ede, and they can be quite aggressive. You've heard how they cheered on 9/11?"

I couldn't contradict him. Perhaps he was right. I could not think of anywhere that looked more peaceful and secure than this pleasant provincial suburb in the center of the Netherlands. But even if he was wrong, and there was no real danger, the fact that they felt so intimidated by the threat of Muslim violence was a sad reflection of what one murder of a public figure could do. From the perspective of a modern European couple, connected to the world through televi-sion and the Internet, Lower Manhattan and Ede were no longer so very far apart, no farther at any rate than the events in Palestine or Iraq were from the Moroccans in dish city who got their news from Casablanca, Beirut, or Qatar.

Even though she had stopped wearing a headscarf, a bit guiltily, in order to conform, Ayaan was still a pious Muslim when she lived in Ede. Her "Dutch mother" had to be care-ful about her dietary restrictions, and Ayaan never touched alcohol. This was confided to me in the kitchen. When we were rejoined by Ayaan, she and her "Dutch parents" laughed about shared memories, but once or twice I noticed a certain awkwardness, perhaps about things better left unspoken. Not everything about her experience in Ede had been positive. There was the painful matter of Ayaan's younger sister, Haweya, the rebel who had worn short skirts in Kenya, the clever one who took a secretarial course and then a job for the United Nations, against her mother's will. She, too, sought to escape from an unwanted marriage, and joined Ayaan in Ede.

Things went well at first. Haweya learned to speak fluent Dutch in less than two years. But it was as if a life of rebelliousness had taken too heavy a toll. After years of taking the lead, of being ahead of Ayaan in striking out for freedom and independence, she began to retreat even as Ayaan started to feel more at home in the West. Just as Ayaan was discarding her headscarf, Haweya began to wear one. Ayaan was making Dutch friends while her sister withdrew into herself, lying in bed, refusing to eat, watching television for hours. She would have fits of crying, and felt ashamed of having upset her mother. Islam was the way back home, to security, salvation, away from this cold, shallow country. Standing in the freezing cold one day, she turned to Ayaan and said: "Do you know why these people don't believe in hell? They're already living in it."[4]

It was terrible for Ayaan to see her sister turn out this way. Just as the freedom of the West was in sight, her sister started yearning for life in the cage. A similar disillusion came over

Ayaan when she worked in shelters for battered Muslim wives. Instead of seeing their own culture and religion as the sources of their misery, as Ayaan did, these women often embraced Islam as their only anchor in an otherwise hopeless existence.

When her sister finally returned to Kenya, after suffering a nervous breakdown, she was told to study the Koran, and sorcerers were brought in to exorcise her demons. When she had fits, she was beaten into submission. Paranoia set in, and she stopped eating. In 1998 she died. It was the most difficult moment in Ayaan's life. Her father told her it was the will of God. But this was becoming harder for her to accept. The knowledge that some women, perhaps many women, couldn't break their bonds, even under the most favorable circumstances, filled her with disappointment, but also with disgust—a disgust she was not always able to disguise when she met such women face to face.

7.

Ayaan only hinted at the guilt she felt when she discarded the chains that bound her to her own past: the scarf, the ban on alcohol, chastity, and dietary rules. Her conversion from the Muslim faith to a flinty atheism did not take place at once. While studying political science at Leiden University, she lived with a Dutch boyfriend called Marco. The most important taboo had been broken. Their relationship ended, however. He was punctual and orderly, while Ayaan was, in her word, "unstructured." Though increasingly doubtful, she was still a Muslim believer.

Marco was not a believer in any religion. When he gave her a copy of a book called *The Atheist Manifesto*, written by a Dutch philosophy professor named Herman Philipse, she refused to read it. Such a document had to be the devil's work, she thought. Four years later, when she was sharing rooms with a young Christian woman from Ede, she asked Marco to send her the manifesto again. This was one year after 9/11. Doubts in Ayaan's mind had provoked arguments with her roommate, who stuck to her faith. On holiday in Greece, Ayaan finally read the manifesto. It posed all the questions she had been asking herself. "I was ready for it now," she wrote later. "I saw that God was a fiction and that submission to his will is surrendering to the will of the strongest."[5]

No longer an anchor (or chain) of security, Islam, for Ayaan, had become "*the* problem." She wrote: "We must face the facts and give migrants what they lack in their own culture: individual dignity. Young Muslim girls in the Netherlands, who still have a spark in their eyes, need not go through what I did."

Holland is a small country. Herman Philipse and I had played in the same sandpit at a kindergarten in The Hague. I remembered him as a somewhat pompous child who spoke with great conviction even then. Tall and handsome, with a taste for bow ties and French phrases, he cuts a rather quaint figure, a kind of nineteenth-century gentleman, the sort of man who likes to personify the high European civilization of the French Enlightenment, equally at home in drawing rooms of The Hague and the high tables of Oxford, where he also teaches.

It was, in its way, a perfect match: the rebellious daughter of a Somali democrat, with the elegant bearing of an aristocrat, and the smooth Dutch professor of philosophy, who could hold forth most eloquently about all the values that she aspired to: Reason, Order, and Freedom—of conscience, speech, and enterprise. That they had a rather public love affair would not be worthy of mention were it not that intellectual, political, and sexual liberty were intimately linked in Ayaan's mind. Her encounter with Philipse's words and person offered her a membership in that self-appointed elite, the public defenders of the Enlightenment. Like all converts, she did not take her membership lightly. As did her comrade-in-arms, Afshin Ellian, she soon felt as though she were surrounded in her adopted land by men and women who had fallen so deeply into the pit of moral decadence that they could never be counted on in the war against the forces of darkness.

8.

It was of the Enlightenment that she spoke when we first met in Paris, moving from café to café, infuriating her Dutch bodyguards. She began by admonishing me for having written in a magazine article about her harsh experiences, as though they explained anything about her views. Her arguments, she said, not without reason, had to be judged on their own merits. They were based on her reading of Karl Popper, she explained, and Spinoza, and Hayek, and Norbert Elias. She was in her element at the Café de Flore, basking in the early summer sunshine, watching the young men and women go by in their thin summer clothes, holding hands, kissing, and generally carrying on in pursuit of private pleasures. "Coming from a tribal world," she said, "it was so good to read books about individuals as social beings."

Islam was *the* problem, but there was hope, she believed, even for the women in Saudi Arabia, where they can't even drive cars. For there were "shortcuts" to the Enlightenment. It didn't have to take hundreds of years. All you needed to do was "free yourself intellectually." The great thing about the Enlightenment, she said, with a spark of almost religious fervor in her eyes, was that "it strips away culture, and leaves only the human individual."

It takes courage for an African immigrant in Europe to say that, even if she is from a privileged class. For a man like Herman Philipse, secure of his rightful place at the high table of European civilization, it is easier to dismiss culture in this way, for there is much that he can take for granted. There is no need for shortcuts if you are educated to believe in universality and individualism; they are products of the civilization to which Philipse was born. Not that this idea of civilization is universally shared in the West. Ayaan's individualism made the social-democratic PVDA an odd party to choose as the platform for her political career. She was attracted to the Social Democrats because of their "social conscience," but culture, for them, was all-important; the "identity" of immigrants in a multicultural society had to be protected, even encouraged. To Ayaan this was nothing less than a *trahison des clercs*.

Her dream of liberation for the Muslims in the West is sabotaged, she believes, "by the Western cultural relativists with their anti-racism offices, who say: 'If you're critical of Islam, you're a racist, or an Islamophobe, or an Enlightenment fundamentalist.' Or: 'It's part of their culture, so you musn't take it away.' This way, the cage will never be broken. Westerners who live off dispensing public welfare, or development aid, or representing minority interests, have made a satanic pact with Muslims who have an interest in preserving the cage."[6]

What makes Ayaan Hirsi Ali such a fascinating and controversial figure is her role in a European civil war that has raged, intellectually and sometimes bloodily, for many centuries, the war between collectivism and individualism, the ideal of universal rights and values versus the pull of the tribal soil, the Enlightenment versus the Counter-Enlightenment, spirit of faith versus enlightened self interest, the hero versus the merchant. Hearing Ayaan talk reminded me sometimes of Margaret Thatcher: the same unyielding intelligence, the same impatience with those from a similar background who lack the wherewithal to "make it," and the same fascination with America. When refugees from Nazi Germany and Austria fled to Britain in the late 1930s, the more conservative ones, who admired the dense network of English traditions, settled there, while the radicals usually moved on to the more rugged terrain of the U.S. Ayaan Hirsi Ali is clearly a radical.

"Ah, yes," she said at the Café de Flore, when I asked her about America, "I feel at home in New York, where you see people of all colors. Some are so black they're almost blue. And there are a lot of people of color who do very well, which simply confirms that there is nothing genetic about success."

It was only to be expected, then, that Ayaan would leave the Social Democrats to join the free enterprise party, the VVD. Delighted to have a beautiful black critic of the welfare state and Muslim radicalism in a party that was, overall, very male and very white, she was welcomed as a walking Statue of Liberty. But this move alienated her even further from the progressives on the Left, who saw her now not just as an enemy of multiculturalism, but as a renegade as well. It gave rise to the common slur that Ayaan was the darling of middle-aged conservative white men—professors of Enlightenment philosophy, guardians of European values, advocates for the rights of Dutch "natives" who live in fear of the alien threat.

In fact, she was too radical for the VVD too. The leaders of this typical party of *regenten* hate nothing more than rocking the boat, and that is precisely what Ayaan was aiming to do. She was always more an activist than a politician, and the compromises and deals that are the bread and butter of politicians were not for her. Like Pim Fortuyn, or Van Gogh, she wanted to stir things up. Her real ambition was to be the Voltaire of Islam, to attack the faith, *écraser l'infame*. "What Muslim culture needs," she wrote, are "books, soaps, poems, and songs that show what's what and mock the religious rules. . . ." What was needed, in her view, was a film like *Life of Brian,* the British spoof on Jesus Christ. What was needed was a movie about the prophet Mohammed, directed by an Arab Theo van Gogh.

8.

I met Funda Müjde, the Turkish-Dutch actress, cabaret artiste, and newspaper columnist, at a café in Amsterdam-Noord, an old working-class district across the bay from the Central Station. Her father had worked there once, living in makeshift barracks for Turkish guest workers, named the Atatürk Camp. He arrived in the 1960s, in search of a better, more independent life, and education for his children. Before he received his work permit in Ankara, a doctor probed his mouth and anus, as though he were a workhorse. Dutch labor recruiters favored illiterate men, who would give less trouble to their new bosses.

Amsterdam-Noord is a district of modest family houses built in the 1920s for workers in the dockyards, now long since defunct. A plaque on one of the houses evokes the renewed hopes of those days, after the mass slaughter of World War I: "The sun of peace had been obscured. The

Czar was murdered, the Kaiser deposed. But here we build and work without pause. . . ."

There is a large new mosque in the midst of the neat little row houses. Bearded men in djellabas stand around the entrance, or sit on benches, conversing in Berber. A few minutes' walk from the mosque is the shelter for abused women, run by Paul Scheerder, a Dutchman who converted to Islam after marrying his Moroccan wife. When I last saw him, he told me how difficult things had been after 9/11, and then again after the murder of Van Gogh, when Muslims were afraid of being spat at or insulted. Officials had become tougher and sometimes abusive, especially, he said, the bureaucrats who were from immigrant families themselves. It was they, the sons of Moroccan or Turkish workers, who deliberately refused to take their shoes off inside people's homes, who trampled over prayer mats, who made an old Egyptian take off his shirt to show his fresh operation scar to make sure he wasn't lying about going off on sick leave. They knew, better than any native Dutch person, all the subtle and not so subtle ways to humiliate a fearful *allochtoon*.

Funda Müjde is a handsome woman with short black hair. Her speech and gestures are those of an Amsterdam actress, quick, slangy, a little theatrical, her words tumbling over one another, not always in the right order. In 2003, she took part in a traveling theater show entitled *Veiled Monologues*. Intimate experiences of Muslim women were retold onstage by a cast of Turkish-Dutch and Moroccan-Dutch actresses, experiences such as losing one's virginity or masturbation, not subjects that Muslim women are used to discussing in public. Ayaan once told me this was one of the most surprising things to her, when she first arrived in the West—the way women talked openly about their sex lives.

The *Veiled Monologues* had been inspired by *The Vagina Monologues*. Aside from the professional cast, well-known Dutch women were invited to read monologues on stage. Ayaan was one of those well-known women.

"A giga-success!" said Funda, which she found delightful but also disturbing. "When it comes to Islam," she explained, "all you need to do is fart to get attention." The other thing that disturbed her was the nature of the audience. Partly because of the high price of a ticket, few Muslim women turned up. The monologues on Muslim lives were performed largely for middle-class non-Muslims. The original idea, to use the stage to start a discussion among Muslims, proved to be an illusion.

Funda admires Ayaan Hirsi Ali, salutes her courage, and yet cannot hide her disapproval, not so much of what she says, but of the way she says it, of her attitude, her style. She tried to explain: "I've lived in Holland much longer than Ayaan. I'm more a part of this society than she is. I've worked with refugees for fourteen years. And I've always resisted the kind of people who cut themselves off from their own kind and then behave arrogantly because they're ashamed of their own background." Listening to these accusations, I thought of the rap group in The Hague and their loathing of the "filthy indigenous clone."

There was an element of one-upmanship here, a kind of competition which Ayaan could not possibly win on the basis of reason. Rivalry among immigrants is not just a matter of age, or birth. One day, on the tram in Amsterdam, I saw a black Surinamese scold an elderly Turkish man who was standing in his way. He berated him for not speaking "proper Dutch like everybody else." In a kebab joint, near the Central Station, I got into a conversation about the European Union with the owner, an Arab from Nazareth. The Dutch, following the French, had just voted against the proposed EU constitution. How had he voted? " 'No,' of course," he replied in fluent, accented Dutch. This was the way he saw it: "Soon, those Turks and other foreigners will want to join Europe, but they're still fifty years behind. We can't afford to wait for *them*."

Funda was aware that Turks in the Netherlands got better press than the Moroccans. This made her feel a bit guilty. But she pointed out that Turks were different from Moroccans. Even among the illiterate Turks, such things as democracy, women's rights, and education for girls were taken for granted. "Turks," she said, "feel a strong sense of superiority. We were always independent, while Morocco was under foreign control."

Although she speaks Turkish and visits Turkey regularly, Funda feels entirely at home in the Netherlands. And yet she has always been aware that "something ugly lurks under the surface." It comes out in the hate mail she receives, especially after she began writing columns for a popular conservative newspaper. Every time she writes something critical about her own country, Holland, she is told to "fuck off back to where you came from!"

Funda didn't hide her indignation; indeed, she acted it out in a flourish of angry gestures. Her hate mail was not always the same, however; the tone had changed with time. "In 2000 I was called a 'filthy Turk.' After 2001, and the rise of Pim Fortuyn, it was 'filthy foreigner [*allochtoon*].' After Hirsi Ali, it was 'filthy Muslim.' " She doesn't blame Ayaan for this. "It's not about her. It's about the Dutch. What's being spat out now, was always there."

Not that Theo van Gogh was like that. Funda worked with him once, in a television soap opera, not unlike *Najib and Julia,* about a Turkish mother (played by Funda) who tries to stop her daughter from seeing a Dutch boyfriend. She adored working with Theo: "He was an absolute sweetie, even though he could say the most terrible things." Theo, she said, could be persuaded to make the Turkish roles more realistic, less like stereotypes. But he had a silly streak: "One day he told me he had smuggled a line into the script that was broadcast without anyone noticing. The line was: 'I fucked Allah.' He was so pleased, just like a child."

9.

Ayaan Hirsi Ali's film *Submission,* directed by Theo van Gogh, is based on the same formula as *Veiled Monologues.* But it goes a step further. When *Veiled Monologues* was first performed in Amsterdam, a poster showing a woman in a see-through black burqa was quickly replaced after Muslim activists threatened to smash the windows of the theater. A new poster showed the same woman, fully covered. The first shot in *Submission* shows a woman about to kneel on a prayer mat. The camera slowly pans from her head down to her toes, revealing her naked body under the diaphanous material of her burqa. Later in the eleven-minute film we see texts from the Koran projected onto the skin of several naked women, texts that point to the submission of women, submission to their fathers, brothers, husbands, and to Allah. For many Muslims, this was a deliberate provocation.

Ayaan would not disagree. She meant it to be provocative. She expected "a section of the Muslim world to come down on me." But "if you want to get a discussion going, and needle people into thinking, you must confront them with dilemmas." Ayaan believes that "anything short of physical and verbal violence should be permissible."[7] It was fine, then, to show a naked woman writhing on the floor, with livid wounds on her back and thighs, talking about being flogged for making love with her boyfriend. Over her wounds we read the words from the Koran: "The woman and the man guilty of adultery or fornication flog each of them with a hundred stripes. . . ."

It was all right to show the naked back of another woman, who tells the story of being raped by her unwanted husband:

> *Undress, he orders me, and I submit*
> *Not to him, but to You.*
> *Lately, enduring my husband is getting harder and*
> *harder.*
> *O, Allah, I pray, give me the strength to endure him*
> *Or I fear*
> *My faith shall weaken.*

Or a third woman, her face swollen and disfigured by bruises from being beaten by her tyrannical husband:

Oh, God, most elevated, submission to Your will assures me of
  a better life in the hereafter,
But I feel the price I pay for my husband's protection and
  maintenance is too high,
I wonder how much longer I will submit.

Or the fourth, raped by her uncle in her own home, and
then abandoned when she is pregnant, knowing she will be
killed by her father for bringing shame to the family:

Oh, Allah, giver and taker of life.
You admonish all who believe to turn towards You in order to
  attain bliss.
I have done nothing my whole life but turn to You.
And now that I pray for salvation, under my veil,
  You remain silent as the grave I long for.
I wonder how much longer I will be able to submit.

Her closest friends advised her against making this film.
They thought nothing good could possibly come of it. But
Ayaan had an answer to all doubters and critics, which deserves respect, if nothing else. She wrote: "In the long history of Jews and Christians searching for enlightenment,
there are bound to have been people who called the strategy
of analyzing sacred texts—to show how ridiculous, cruel, or
unjust they were—counterproductive. I copied my strategy

from the Judeo-Christian criticism of faith-based absolutism. That is how *Submission Part I** must be seen. How effective my chosen strategy is should be clear to anyone who knows the history of Western criticism of religion."

It is hard to disagree in principle. Whether she was wise is another matter. But wisdom is not always the quickest way to necessary change. Those who dare to challenge the dogmas that justify oppression are not always wise. Resistance is not always wise. But it can be necessary. The problem in the case of Ayaan's film is the intended target. She wrote it in English, so it must have been meant for an international audience. Theo van Gogh spoke of trying to sell it to the Arabic television station Al Jazeera, a bold but astonishingly naive idea. If the film was intended for the ayatollahs of Iran, or the imams of Saudi Arabia, or the patriarchs in Rif mountain villages, the chances they would ever see it were virtually nil. The film was shown only on a highbrow cultural program on Dutch TV. In this limited context, Ayaan Hirsi Ali was no Voltaire. For Voltaire had flung his insults at the Catholic Church, one of the two most powerful institutions of eighteenth-century France, while Ayaan risked offending only a minority that was already feeling vulnerable in the heart of Europe.

It was intended to be a comedy. That is what Van Gogh

---

* Part II was never made, but Hirsi Ali still insists that one day it will be.

had suggested to Ayaan when they met in Amsterdam to discuss her plans. She had something else in mind, to design an exhibition with life-sized puppets, illustrating the brutalities in the Koran. But perhaps with the *Veiled Monologues* in mind, Ayaan ended up writing *Submission*. It was always her idea. Van Gogh gave her technical assistance, but lamented the lack of humor. It was too preachy for his taste. But even as a sermon, it didn't really work. Ayaan made it too easy for people to miss the point.

Even Samir, the sophisticated young architect I met in Rotterdam, missed the point, but in a revealing way. Ayaan's take on the role of women in Islam was totally wrong, he said. "Just look and see what happens if anyone insults our mothers; any Moroccan male would go berserk." True enough. But this is something a Sicilian might have said too, or indeed anyone from a clannish, rural society where men rule and women are either holy mothers or whores. Samir was probably right, also, when he observed that Ayaan's criticisms were more about culture than religion per se, and he conceded that she had some valid points. But to him, religion was a distraction; to her, it was the main point.

Nora, the head of the Union of Islamic Students at Nijmegen University, was watching television at home with her mother on the night of the broadcast. While zapping from channel to channel, her mother heard the sounds of Muslim prayer. Astonished to hear this on Dutch TV, she was curious. "But as soon as she saw the naked body of a woman with texts from the Koran, she was stunned. I know that Ayaan wanted to shock. But my mother wasn't even ready for that. She just thought it was uncouth for a woman to be praying in that state."

Nora was not so much offended herself, she claimed, as "embarrassed," embarrassed for her mother's sake, so she switched to another channel. Perhaps, she said, "we will be ready to have a debate like this in twenty years' time, when we are on a more equal footing. But it's too soon. The first generation isn't ready to face this kind of thing."

This was the most generous assessment I heard from any Muslim of Ayaan's film, and Nora was more religious than many I spoke to. But she was wrong about the generational aspect. It was precisely the children of immigrants, the second generation, people of Nora's age, who couldn't contain their rage. The sense of inequality is part of this, inequality common to all minorities. But the problem goes deeper, to another inequality: between immigrants who have the education, the intelligence, the social connections, and the ambition, to do well as individuals and assimilate, and the more vulnerable ones who need a collective identity to cling to. This has been true of Jews. It has been the story of new immigrants in the history of the United States. You can see the same story being played out in Europe today.

Critics of Ayaan Hirsi Ali usually quote one particular television program to show what they believe is wrong with her approach. Ayaan has always shown a great interest in women who seek refuge from their abusive men in secret shelters, known as "lay off my body homes" (*blijf van m'n lijf huis*). These women have already taken a bold step that passive victims cannot face; they had the courage to escape. If Ayaan has a natural constituency anywhere for her battle against Muslim machismo, these bruised housewives and battered daughters should be it.

A well-known news program decided it would be a good idea to show *Submission* at one of these shelters and then film a discussion with Ayaan. Four young women watched the film together. A number of them had seen it before. Only one would show her face; the others feared repercussions. They all spoke perfect Dutch.

Their first reaction was defensive: How could Ayaan be so deliberately insulting, they asked. The naked women were a sign of disrespect. Ayaan was only "using" the film, they believed. She was only "playing with Islam" to further her own ends. Working with a man like Van Gogh, they all agreed, was bound to cause offense.

Ayaan answered, very politely, that it was her right as a

Muslim, indeed her duty, to criticize what was bad about Islam, and the oppression of women was one of those bad things. The unveiled woman sitting next to Ayaan got agitated, tugging at her yellow sweater. One of the women agreed that women were oppressed, but this was because of culture and education, and had nothing to do with the Koran. Ayaan repeated that she had quoted from the sacred texts. But that's not the point, cried the women: "You're just insulting us. My faith is what strengthened me. That's how I came to realize that my situation at home was wrong."

"This must stop!" said one of the women, whose face was disguised. "You must stop." Ayaan said she would never stop. "You must stop! If you can't see that you're hurting me, I can't continue this discussion!" Okay, said Ayaan, with a dismissive wave of her hand, "so long then."

It was this wave, this gentle gesture of disdain, this almost aristocratic dismissal of a noisome inferior, that upset her critics more than anything. Recalling the meetings with Ayaan and other Muslim feminists, Funda said that Ayaan was incapable of listening. With Ayaan, she said, "I sensed aggression, a hatred almost, for the kind of people she was trying to save."

This is going too far, but there is perhaps, in this recent immigrant, this daughter of the Somali elite, something that is quite *regent*-esque, despite her objections to the pampering welfare state. Ayaan is, in her way, a bit like a Dutch no-table, who would not have looked entirely out of place in a portrait by Frans Hals—apart from being black, that is. Her words bear repeating: "We must . . . give migrants what they lack in their own culture: individual dignity." The sentiment is good, even noble, but rather too much *de haut en bas*. You cannot "give" people individual dignity. It is theirs by right, even if they find it in their faith.

And so Ayaan Hirsi Ali ended up preaching to those who were already convinced, and further alienating many of those whom she needed to engage. Although only eleven min-utes long, and shown just once, *Submission* had an impact that was at least as important as that of *Zo is het,* the televi-sion program that outraged so many Christians almost ex-actly forty years ago. But *Submission* was no joke, nor did it challenge the beliefs of a complacent majority, the main-stream of a secure and prosperous European nation. It did not even speak for a generation. That it would cause offense was clear, but even those who agreed with its sentiments could not predict its murderous consequences. Certainly not Theo van Gogh.

Interviewed after the showing of the film, Van Gogh hailed the courage of Ayaan. "People who call her reckless," he said, "are cowards. Bombs haven't gone off. I haven't been threatened. I don't feel threatened in the least." But he also said something else to Ayaan, which was at once weirdly insouciant and perceptive. Nobody would harm him, he assured her, "because I'm just the village idiot. It's you who should be worried, for you're the apostate." What he hadn't realized was that the jester can lose his license, that he wasn't living in a village anymore, even in cool, swinging Amsterdam.

SIX

A Promising Boy

"Wow," he said. It was July 12, 2005, the last day of Mohammed Bouyeri's trial. "Mohammed B." in the Dutch press, "Mo" to his friends, was charged with the murder of Theo van Gogh, the attempted murder of several policemen, threatening Ayaan Hirsi Ali, and terrorizing the Dutch population.

"Wow" was almost the first word Mohammed, a pudgy man in a dark djellaba, had uttered during his trial. He refused to be defended or to defend himself in a court whose authority he didn't recognize. Only God's laws, the Shariah, were the true laws. At the beginning of the trial, he confirmed his name. The rest of the time, in the stark, modern courtroom in an Amsterdam suburb, Mohammed smiled thinly, tugged at his wispy beard, adjusted his wire-rimmed glasses, and fiddled with his pen. Just once, when the presiding judge, Udo Bentinck, wondered why the defendant had turned his back on a society that offered him complete freedom to follow his faith, did he allow himself to snap into a moment of anger. He shouted: "In the the name of Allah, the merciful bringer of mercy." And then in Dutch: "I worship Allah every day and pray that he protects me from ever changing the way I think now."

That was it, until that "wow," an Americanism that crept into the language of the young in the 1960s and somehow got lodged there. "Wow" was like the Nike sneakers that Mohammed wore under his black djellaba, the badge of global youth, nurtured on American street culture. Wrapped around his head like a turban was a black and white kaffiyeh, the Palestinian scarf made famous by Chairman Arafat. Theo van Gogh had posed in a similar scarf for the cover photograph of one of his books, entitled *Allah Knows Better*. Van Gogh meant to mock, while Mohammed, perhaps no less theatrically, was mimicking the style of the seventh-century prophet.

"What did you say?" asked the judge.

"I said 'wow,' you wrote very nicely. So I can say something now, and you won't interrupt me? Can I say critical things here too?"

The judge told him to go ahead. And Mohammed made one of the most astonishing speeches ever heard in a Dutch courtroom. He spoke slowly, in halting sentences, in an accent that was mostly Amsterdam with a Moroccan-Dutch lilt. First he addressed Theo van Gogh's mother, Anneke. He could not "feel her pain," he said, for he didn't know what it was like "to lose a child born through such pain and so many tears." Because he was not a woman, and because she was an infidel.

It was not his intention, he said, to give a political speech. But he wanted her to know that he didn't kill her son because he (Theo) was Dutch, or because he, Mohammed, felt insulted as a Moroccan. Theo was no hypocrite, he continued, for he had simply spoken his mind. "So the story that I felt insulted as a Moroccan, or because he called me a goat fucker, that is all nonsense. I acted out of faith. And I made it clear that if it had been my own father, or my little brother, I would have done the same thing." As far as his state of mind was concerned, he could assure the court that "if I were ever released, I would do exactly the same, exactly the same."

He explained to the court that he was obligated to "cut off the heads of all those who insult Allah and his prophet" by the same divine law that didn't allow him "to live in this country, or in any country where free speech is allowed." Alas, there was no country where people like him could seek refuge, so he had had no choice but to live in the Netherlands.

To the policemen who arrested him, he said that he had shot at them "fully intending to kill them, and to be killed." This statement unleashed an extraordinary outburst of emotion among the policemen. Tears ran down their cheeks as they fell into each other's arms. Heads were stroked and backs patted. They were traumatized, so it was reported, kept awake by nightmares, and had frequent fits of crying. The idea of a suicidal killer in the middle of Amsterdam was just too much to bear.

Unperturbed, Mohammed finished his speech with the following words: "You can send all your psychologists and all your psychiatrists, and all your experts, but I'm telling you, you will never understand. You cannot understand. And I'm telling you, if I had the chance to be freed and the chance to repeat what I did on the second of November, *wallahi* [by Allah] I'm telling you, I would do exactly the same."

"That is all you wanted to say?" asked the judge.

"I'm not here to feel sorry for myself," Mohammed concluded, "or to blame anyone. Perhaps this could be a small consolation to Mrs. van Gogh. That is all. For the rest, I really don't care."

"Every little bit helps," muttered Anneke van Gogh after the trial.

The judge had no choice but to sentence Mohammed Bouyeri to a lifetime in prison.

It had been a most peculiar trial, which invited odd behavior. Theo's ex-wife, on her first sight of Mohammed, exclaimed to her husband's murderer: "Look, Mo, the same scarf!" and pointed to Van Gogh's cover photo.

Mohammed's lawyer, Peter Plasman, looked glum most of the time. It cannot have been easy to defend a client who didn't wish to be defended and told the judge he would commit murder again at the first opportunity.

The Friends of Theo gave their impressions of the trial on television. They were disappointed, they said, for the killer was clearly unworthy of his victim. Theodor Holman thought it "was a tragedy that the man who killed Theo was such a lackluster fellow, so devoid of any spirit." Theo's producer, Gijs van de Westelaken, added that Mohammed was so small.

The most emotional declaration in the courtroom came from Anneke van Gogh, who also pointed out the killer's lack of stature. "A loser," she called him, "but a loser who committed homicide." Not just that, but a loser who "had lived on welfare for three years," a loser who got off on watching videos of murder and mutilations, a loser who was convinced that his god commanded him "to kill the pig." Well, there would be no paradise for him, she said, and no seventy-two virgins either.

Theo, her beloved son, was murdered because of his ideas. She quoted from one of Mohammed's tracts: "No discussions, no demonstrations, no petitions, no marches. Only death will separate lies from truth." This didn't bode well, she said, for a country "where the works of Voltaire, Molière, Victor Hugo, and Jonathan Swift were published during the seventeenth and eighteenth centuries, because they were banned in their own countries." Theo, she said, was a brave exponent of that tradition, our contemporary Voltaire or Swift.

So it was back to the Enlightenment again. Leon de Winter, the Jewish novelist who had so often borne the brunt of Van Gogh's personal venom, declared in the *Wall Street Journal* that the nation of Spinoza and Erasmus was dead. When we had tea in her Wassenaar garden, Anneke van Gogh gave me a short exposition on the nature of Islam. It was "a fossilized religion," she believed, which had "never had an Enlightenment." Moroccans were in a "state of denial" after the murder, because "that's in their culture, their macho culture. They are incapable of self-criticism."

This had become the received opinion, repeated like a mantra by a large number of public commentators, experts, and politicians. But it hardly addressed the question that was on everyone's mind during the trial of Mohammed Bouyeri. Why did a young man, who was neither poor nor oppressed, who had received a decent education, a man who had never had trouble making friends, who enjoyed smoking dope and drinking beer, why would such a man turn into a holy warrior whose only wish was to kill, and perhaps more mysteriously, to die? It was the same question people asked after the bombings in the London underground, set off by similar young men, who played cricket, had girlfriends, went to the pub. All we know is that they murdered in the name of Allah and his prophet. Quite *why* they did it is harder to explain.

2.

The expert witness on Islam during Mohammed Bouyeri's trial was Professor Ruud Peters. He had analyzed Mohammed's writings—letters, articles in his neighborhood paper, texts posted on Internet websites. The story he uncovered is one of an increasingly disturbed young man whose conversion to jihadism took place over little more than one year. Peters explained that Mohammed had begun by rejecting "Western values." This would have been around February 2003. The next stage, reached in October, was his rejection of the democratic state and its legal institutions. Then, in March 2004, he called for a global jihad against democracy. Finally, in July, he advocated violence against individuals who had insulted Islam or the Prophet.

Much of Mohammed's writing has the air of childish fantasy. In March 2004, he announced that soon "the knights of Allah" would march into the houses of parliament and raise "the flag of Tawheed [God's sovereignty]" and transform the parliament into a Shariah court. Other effusions, such as one entitled *This Is the Way*, are soaked in the lurid images of advanced paranoia: "The battle against the Truth has been waged since the beginning of mankind, but it has never been as fierce and massive as in our time. The monsters of the army of satanic powers are ready everywhere to arrest the pronouncers of absolute truth and throw them into their bestial dungeons. Some monsters go so far as to kill the tellers of truth in their own homes. The masses, who seem to be dulled and hypnotized by the great media offensive unleashed by the enemies of Islam on the spirits and souls of the people, are part of the great [in]visible battle."[1]

Most of the religious extremism—snatches of revolutionary texts, calls for jihad, glorifications of martyrdom—was translated from English-language websites. Professor Peters did not think that Mohammed was proficient in Arabic. If he translated anything at all from Arabic, he must have had help, he said.

Peters's report, prepared for the court, makes for strange reading, because he attempts to find coherence in these violent ravings where often there is none. "Ideological and religious development" is a rather grand description of Mohammed's thinking. But the report is worth studying nonetheless, not so much for what it says about Islam, but for what it says about the revolutionary fantasies of a confused and very resentful young man. These are not so different from the fantasies of other confused and resentful young men in the past. You can find them in the novels of Dostoyevsky or Joseph Conrad, desperadoes who imagine themselves as part of a small elite, blessed with moral purity, surrounded by a world of evil. They are obsessed with the idea of violent death as a divinely inspired cleansing agent of worldly corruption. Mohammed Bouyeri is like the Professor in Conrad's *The Secret Agent,* the suicide bomber who is "terrible in the simplicity of his idea," the bomber who will always overcome his enemies, because, in his words, they "depend on life . . . whereas I depend on death, which knows no restraint and cannot be attacked. My superiority is evident."

To call it nihilism would be wrong, for Mohammed did have a utopian ideal, however absurd and cobbled together, which was the state of pure faith, where nothing but the word of Allah and his prophet could penetrate. When he was visited by a prison psychiatrist before his trial, Mohammed turned his back on him, put on his headphones, and drowned out the world in amplified Koranic prayers. The impulse to seek oblivion, to be intoxicated or overwhelmed by a great force, is not rare. The rush of drugs, sex, and death stems from a common source. But this leaves the question, why him? What turned Mohammed into a character from Conrad?

Hamid Bouyeri, Mohammed's father, is a relatively successful man in terrible physical shape. Years of hard menial work in Amsterdam, where he arrived in 1965 via France, have damaged his knees so badly that he can no longer kneel when he goes to pray at his neighborhood mosque. He has to sit in a chair. It can't have been easy to raise a family of eight children in a cramped apartment on the salary of a dishwasher. He worked long hours and did all the shopping on the weekends. His wife barely spoke a word of Dutch. And yet, compared to the people in Douar Ikhammalen, a dirt-poor hamlet in the Rif mountains, where he began tending goats at the age of five, Hamid is a rich man. The mosque near the river, down from the village, with its fine minaret covered in red, yellow, and green mosaic, was built with his money. He also built a house, where his brother lives on a small pension earned from years of backbreaking work in Paris. But Hamid likes to spend his summer holidays in another place he owns, in Oujda, a resort town near the Algerian border with hotels, restaurants, and cafés.

Mohammed last visited his father's native village in 1999, when he traveled through in his white Peugeot. His Berber was not really good enough for him to communicate easily with his relatives, and the tiny village, which most young men left to work in Europe because they could barely make a living growing corn and olives in the hard red clay, held few attractions. He preferred to hang out in Oujda, where he spent most of his time in the cafés, listening to Western pop music.

Much was made in the press, after the murder of Van Gogh, of Mohammed's successful integration as a Dutch citizen. He was said to have been "promising," a "clever kid," a "positivo," who was popular and active in the community. There was some truth to this, but one of his high school teachers also remembers him as "timid and aloof,"[2] a boy who had trouble looking you in the eye. Always on the heavy side, he was no good at sports and shy around girls. He did work very hard, though, for he wanted to do well at school, have a career, be a success.

When Mohammed entered Mondrian High School, it was still a mixed school. About 40 percent of the pupils were of non-Dutch origin, mostly Moroccans. Everyone took part in theater performances, fashion shows, and school excursions. But things began to change while "Mo" was there. Muslim girls were no longer allowed to go on school trips. Boys cut classes and spent their days watching satellite TV, or hanging out in snack bars on nearby August Allebé Square. Within five years, the school had become "black," almost 100 percent *allochtoon*.

A few weeks after Van Gogh's murder I spoke to the head-master of a mixed school in the east of Amsterdam, near the place of the murder. His school had pupils of forty-two different nationalities. When it came to school excursions and other extracurricular activities, it was always the Moroccan parents who objected to sending their daughters, never Turks or other Muslims. Yet the Moroccan girls were also among the hardest-working pupils. "To get away from the influence of their fathers," he explained. I asked him what he thought of Mohammed Bouyeri. Had he come across radicalized youths of that kind?

He answered my question in a roundabout way. "Ten years ago," he said, "we would tell promising pupils from minorities to pull a little harder. We put pressure on them, telling them they had to work harder than others to succeed. Often they would, but then, if things didn't go their way, when they faced a setback, perhaps because of discrimination, they could get very angry indeed."

Something like this appears to have happened with Mohammed Bouyeri. His former history teacher told a newspaper reporter that the radical youths were almost always the better educated: "I think they find ideals in fundamentalism that are impossible for them to reach in Dutch society when they leave school. Because employers won't take on Moroccans, for example."

Apart from his teachers, most of the native Dutch people

Mohammed encountered in his daily life in an immigrants' community were bureaucrats of one kind or another: social workers, welfare officers, local officials who dealt with subsidies for this and that. Many of them have good memories of him, at least initially, as a reasonable person. "Mo" wanted to be a pillar of his community, help people out, by offering them computer lessons, or organizing youth clubs.

An old friend recalled Mo as a cheerful boy, full of curiosity and good stories. They delivered newspapers together and talked about all kinds of things, from soccer to the black holes in the universe. His politics were moderately left-wing. The fate of the Palestinians exercised him, but he didn't get his information from Al Jazeera or Moroccan television. Instead he watched Belgian TV, which he found less biased in favor of Israel than the Dutch stations.[3] Mohammed hardly ever went to the mosque. Fasting during Ramadan was about the extent of his religious life. Friends remember how much fun he was when he got stoned on hash, spinning long fantastic tales from his fertile imagination.

A "positivo," then, but in 1994 came his first disappointment. The youth club which he frequented with his friends had to make way for a new apartment building. Local authorities reassured the boys that they would get a new club soon. The boys asked for a shuttle bus to take them to their new clubhouse, which was only a short walk from the old one. Their demand was turned down. They were then told that the club had to be shared with adults. Since adult company was the last thing they wanted, the final evening in the old club turned sour, with acts of vandalism. When the occasion ended in a small riot, the kids were chased out of the building by dozens of policemen with dogs. There was a rash of arson attacks on the new place. Security had to be tightened.

After graduating from Mondrian High School, Mohammed enrolled in an accounting course. Then, another setback. In November 1997, he got into a brawl with a number of policemen in a coffeeshop in Amsterdam. When he applied for a security job at Schiphol Airport a year later, he was turned down because of a negative police report. Around that same time, resentment that had been seething in the neighborhood ever since the trouble over the clubhouse suddenly exploded into a full-scale riot on August Allebé Square. Bottles were thrown, cars rocked, windows smashed. But Mohammed and his friends were nowhere near the scene. They were getting high in a dance bar north of Amsterdam.

He met his first and possibly only girlfriend there, a half-Dutch, half-Tunisian girl, tall and striking in miniskirts. He was proud to be seen with her. But the affair didn't last long. Attracting women was never easy for Mohammed. He liked typical Dutch girls, perhaps because he thought they were "easy." But he could be too aggressive. On a holiday in the

Canary Islands, his companion, a Moroccan-Dutch friend from Amsterdam, worried when Mohammed tried to pick up Spanish girls in the streets. Rejection made him violent. He would blame it on racism.

The words of the psychiatrist in Amersfoort, Bellari Said, came to mind when I read this. He ascribed the high incidence of schizophrenia among Muslim males in Europe to the "cognitive wiring" that goes wrong when faced with bewildering temptations. While many women embrace the liberties of Western life, men, faced with rejection and frustration, turn away to a fantasy of tribal honor and religious rectitude. A teenage desire for "easy" women makes way for disgust and rage.

The official response to the riot on August Allebé Square was to invest more government money in the neighborhood. The Bouyeri family's apartment was one of the places scheduled for renovation. Mohammed and several friends demanded from the authorities that the apartments be rebuilt in a way that was in line with Islamic custom. The women should be able to go in and out of the kitchen unseen. At least one city councillor was sympathetic. Instead, another disillusion. No renovation. The building was now slated for demolition. In the meantime, social workers dropped in for regular visits to see to the welfare of the families who lived there. Mohammed refused to talk to them.

I have a friend who lives on August Allebé Square, the writer Dubravka Ugresic. Her building, which stands with its back to the square, is better than most. Many of her neighbors are non-Dutch: Chinese, Eastern Europeans, some people from the Middle East. Dubravka found a refuge in Amsterdam from the poisonous nationalism in her native Croatia, or, as she would have preferred it to remain, Yugoslavia. She is a refugee from a country that no longer exists. Cast adrift after the collapse of Communism, she is now part of a new European diaspora. We first met in San Francisco, at a writers' conference in 1990, and have seen one another in various places since. One memorable evening in Berlin, we entered a bar full of Muslim refugees from Bosnia. Dubravka was the only woman, surrounded by agitated mustachioed men who wanted to tell us about all the terrible things they had seen, the rape rooms, the torture camps, the sites of mass killing. We asked them what life was like in the refugee shelter in Berlin. Fine, they said, fine—except for one thing. Oh, and what was that? The Gypsies, they said. They're scum. They should all be killed.

Dubravka was not sentimental. She had acquired her skepticism the hard way. All was quiet on August Allebé Square when we had dinner at her apartment on a midsummer night. Many of the local inhabitants were away on family visits to Turkey and Morocco. While talking about life in Holland, she told me something that I had heard once before, from Ayaan Hirsi Ali, about the public generosity and the private conformism of the Dutch. The generosity of the state toward refugees and other newcomers can lead to a peculiar resentment. The Dutch feel, in Ayaan's words, that since they "have been so kind" to the foreigners, the foreigners should behave as the Dutch do. Then there is the other kind of resentment, of the recipients of Dutch government largesse, who feel that it is never enough. Dubravka described the behavior of people from the Balkan countries. "They develop a criminal mentality in Holland," she said. "They think this country is a soft touch." A bit like those "easy" women.

Europeans are proud of their welfare states, but they were not designed to absorb large numbers of immigrants. Immigrants appear to fare better in the harsher system of the United States, where there is less temptation to milk the state. The necessity to fend for oneself encourages a kind of tough integration. It is for this reason, perhaps, that immigrants from Africa or the Caribbean often express a contempt for African-Americans, who feel, for understandable historic reasons, that the state owes them something. Immigrants cannot afford to feel that kind of entitlement in the U.S. But in Europe at least some of them do.

Reliance on state subsidies, even when it is utterly justified, has another pernicious effect on immigrant life. Organizations that use public money to represent the interests of minorities, or immigrants who work for the government, are often suspected of venality and self-promotion. Their motives, however selfless, are seen as tainted by the proximity of officialdom. "The subsidy tap" is a phrase I heard over and over from Moroccan-Dutch citizens, always used with scorn. To drink from that tap is to run the risk of becoming a "Moroccan mascot" or "pampered Muslim."

When I asked a prison imam of Moroccan origin about Forum, the worthy organization that promotes multiculturalism and tolerance, he rolled his eyes and said that Forum was "a subsidy tap which should be turned off." In fact, he said, he was against subsidies. "Muslims always want subsidies. This should stop. The welfare state has gone too far."

The prison imam, Ali Eddaoudi, is not some braying free-marketeer, but a tough young activist, in his words, "a man of sharp opinions." He was "proud" of his Muslim "brothers" for staging boycotts and demonstrations against the Danish cartoons mocking the Prophet. This he saw as a spirited defense of "religious civilization." Muslims, on the other hand, who had made a successful leap into the mainstream of Dutch politics were treated with scorn. The typical Muslim politician, he would have me know, was a "model alien."

Such people were not to be trusted. Instead, the political parties should "find more people who are part of their own communities." I suspected that he meant more people like himself. So I asked him. He replied that he didn't stand a chance in politics: "Just my beard is enough to scare them off."

5.

Like many young men, Mohammed Bouyeri had an authority problem. But it was not quite the same problem that commonly afflicts the native-born *autochtoon*. If confrontations with the paternalistic authorities are felt as a humiliation, the lack of parental authority at home can be just as bad, or worse. Nora, the Muslim student leader in Nijmegen, felt "embarrassed" for her mother when they watched *Submission* on TV. Samir, the architect in Rotterdam, cringed when he saw the lack of respect for his father at work. Farhane, the actor in The Hague, felt the helplessness of his parents, who didn't know how to cope with the simplest tasks in Dutch life.

Mohammed's conflict with his father was common enough in immigrant families from rural backgrounds. It concerned honor, family honor, and it involved sexual freedom. In the spring of 2000, his seventeen-year-old sister Wardia met a boyfriend, named Abdu, a neighborhood kid, part of a gang of Moroccan youths known as the Daltons, a name lifted from a popular Belgian comic strip, read by most Dutch children, about a cowboy called Lucky Luke. The Daltons had been in trouble with the police. But that was not what bothered Mohammed. His problem was his father's lack of authority. He should have kept Wardia under control. Having a boyfriend before marriage was not permissible. The fact that Mohammed had had a girlfriend himself was irrelevant, or perhaps not irrelevant but an example of faulty cognitive wiring. He was a man. Dutch women were easy, and therefore, in fact, disgusting. In the case of his sister, family honor was impugned. "What can I do?" said the father. "She won't listen to me."

Mohammed wouldn't let Abdu in the house. A fight broke out. The police had to be called to restore order. Soon after that, Mohammed left home, rented an apartment, and refused to see his father for more than a year. Around that time he also switched his studies from accountancy to corporate information technology. A year later, Mohammed was arrested again. He had come across Abdu in a park in the center of Amsterdam. Egged on by another Moroccan-Dutch youth, they had a nasty fight. When the police arrived, Mohammed had a buck knife in his hand, which he used to threaten one of the cops, a man of Turkish origin. The first time he lunged at him, he missed by inches. The second time, he slashed the policeman's neck.

Barely free, after twelve weeks in jail, another blow. Mohammed's mother died of breast cancer. He had been her favorite child. Despite his periodic tantrums, Mohammed was good at hiding his feelings. He didn't attend her funeral in Morocco, and the effect of her death on him was not immediately apparent to others. But people who knew him well thought he had become more introspective. He wanted to "find the truth," he later wrote in a farewell letter to his family, just before he murdered Van Gogh. "I have often tried to find ways of showing you the Truth, but it's as though there was always a wall between us."

This quest for the truth set him on the path to Islam. Some would blame his domineering behavior toward his sister on Islam too. Certainly Ayaan Hirsi Ali would. But religion was perhaps not the primary issue. More important was the question of authority, of face, in a household where the father could give little guidance, and in a society from which a young Moroccan male might find it easier to receive subsidies than respect.

Mohammed's quest for the truth might also have been affected by 9/11, but this event appears to have confused him more than anything else. He certainly didn't support the U.S. government, but he didn't condone the killing of innocent civilians either. Violence, he told friends, was not the solution. On the other hand, he was open to the idea that it was the Jews who had staged the attacks. But this was hardly unusual. Many Muslims were receptive to that particular canard.

Mohammed was still active in neighborhood projects, organizing public debates, cooking lessons, and the like. He had plans to organize a new youth club in his old school. It would be called Mondriaans Doenia, or Mondrian's World. A photograph taken at this time, published in the neighborhood paper, shows a friendly young man stroking his sparse beard while smiling at the camera. His old habits—the beer drinking, the dope smoking, the chasing after Dutch girls— were gradually giving way to an increasingly moralistic outlook, especially after this latest plan, too, came to nothing. There were already enough other youth clubs, he was told. There wasn't enough money to build a new one.

Mohammed's interest in corporate information technology proved to be as fleeting as his interest in bookkeeping, so he changed once again, this time to something called social educational relief work. He received a scholarship for this new field of study, but soon got bored again. Fellow students noticed a peculiar priggishness about him. He threatened people who drank alcohol, for example. One student recalled that "he didn't seem to have any real friends at the

college, especially at the end, when he formed a separate little group with other people who are now in jail."[4]

Although he still attended meetings of his neighborhood
committee, Mohammed's moods darkened. He shouted
people down, refused to shake hands with women, broke up
meetings with loud prayers or incantations to Allah, and
blamed the failure of getting a subsidy for Mondriaans
Doenia on prejudice against Muslims. He changed his appearance as well. Not only had he grown a beard, but a
Moroccan djellaba and prayer hat were now part of his usual
dress, instead of jeans. Old friends were dropped. A curt
"salaam" was all they got when they encountered him in the
street. New friends, such as an illegal immigrant from
Morocco named Nouredine, came into his life. There was
also a younger man, called Samir, who had attended the
same school as Mohammed. Samir had left for Chechnya,
aged seventeen, to join the holy war, but soon came back because he couldn't stand the cold. Perhaps assuming that the
sun shone everywhere south of Holland, he had taken only
summer clothes. One of his teachers at school called him a
"doltish Robin Hood."

It was Nouredine who introduced Mohammed to a new
source of authority, one that seemed more welcoming, more
authentic, more sustaining, than anything he had experienced
before. His father was now an estranged figure, who repre-

sented weakness and defeat. Officials of the Dutch welfare state, Mohammed felt, had all let him down, out of impotence or treachery, or possibly even hatred of Islam. But here, finally, was the real thing: a wise man from the East, who would give meaning to his life, and justification to his resentments.

Mohammed Radwan Alissa, also known as Abou Khaled, was a radical Muslim preacher who had fled Assad's secular dictatorship in Syria in 1995. Flying to Frankfurt on a false passport, he failed to get asylum in Germany. He had heard that Holland was a easier place to operate illegally, so he quickly crossed the border and began to preach to small groups in the backrooms of provincial shops, or in private apartments. His message was an extreme form of Islamic purism known as Takfir. According to this doctrine, Muslims who depart from the true faith and fail to live by divine laws must be declared infidels, and deserve to be killed by true believers. Since democracy, or indeed any form of secular government, is an affront to true belief, Muslims who take part in such systems are by definition infidels.

Abou Khaled, a tall man who wore a black jacket over his white djellaba and spoke Dutch with a German accent, was preaching in a store called the Internet Phonehouse, in Schiedam, a small town near Rotterdam, when Mohammed was introduced to him by Nouredine. The fact that Abou Khaled preached only in Arabic, which was hard for Mohammed to follow, might have added to his mystique.

For here was a man from the heartland of Islam, and not some traditionalist graybeard from the Rif mountains who went through the motions of Islam and barely spoke Arabic, or some wishy-washy immigrant imam currying favors with the Dutch authorities. Abu Khaled was a man of pure faith, a revolutionary, a modern prophet who could show him the way to the Truth.

The disciples who clustered around the Syrian preacher at these secretive get-togethers were mostly little more than kids, like Samir and Mohammed, confused kids who were so impressed that they called him "the Sheik." Once they got acquainted, Mohammed asked the Sheik to come to his apartment in Amsterdam and talk to his circle of friends about the Koran. The Sheik, said one of these young disciples, was "so wise that he knew five times as much as Mohammed Bouyeri."

By the middle of 2003, Mohammed had retreated into the narrow world of a few like-minded friends and his computer. Dutch intelligence would brand this group, which also included two brothers, Jason and Jaime, born of an American father and Dutch mother, the Hofstad Group, or Royal Court City Group, after the common name for The Hague, where several of the members lived. Jason and Jaime had plans to blow up the houses of parliament. There were possible links with jihadist organizations in Spain and other European countries. Mohammed became the house intel-

lectual, as it were, of the Hofstad Group. He posted ideological tracts on websites, using the name Abu Zubair.

The friends, and sometimes the Sheik himself, met at
Mohammed's apartment and played DVDs on his laptop,
downloaded from Islamist websites or passed on by other en-
thusiasts. They showed executions in the Middle East, foreign infidels having their throats cut by holy warriors
wrapped in scarves and balaclavas. Mohammed, according to
a man who attended these sessions, got visibly excited by
these grisly spectacles. Nouredine spent his wedding night on
a mattress in Mohammed's apartment, together with his
bride, watching infidels being slaughtered.[5]

Mohammed's language became steadily more violent.
"The Shariah," he wrote, "is a sacred independent sover-
eign system for life that cannot be under the authority of a
false human system. Indeed, the Shariah has come to wipe
this type of system from the face of the earth." This was in
October 2003. In February 2004, his tone was even fiercer:
"To withdraw from the infidels means hating them, being
their enemy, being revolted by them, loathing them, and
fighting them." Even a good Muslim, he said, who prays,
eats halal food, goes on pilgrimage to Mecca and calls for
jihad, even such a person, "if he feels no hatred for the enemies of Islam, becomes an infidel, even if he only loved one
of them and this person was a relative."

This is the upside-down world of Takfir, where to love

is a sin, and to hate is a virtue. The Dutch police, tipped off about the Hofstad Group, raided some of their usual meeting places and arrested five members, including the Syrian. Mohammed was not among them, for the secret service saw him as nothing more than a peripheral figure. So Mohammed delivered pizzas to the jail where his friends were held and shouted abuse at the guards. Since no actual crime had been committed, the prisoners were soon released. In the spring of 2004, Abou Khaled was a regular visitor again at Mohammed's apartment. But there was a difference between the Sheik and his disciple. Abou Khaled had no direct interest in the Netherlands. His mind was in the Middle East. Mohammed, in a perverse way, remained remarkably Dutch.

6.

There are people who believe that the terror of political Islam would go away if only the problems of the Middle East were solved. If only the Americans would withdraw their troops from Iraq, and Israel would be forced to allow Palestinians to reclaim their land, if only Western governments and corporations would stop propping up dictators, if only the bloody stain of colonialism could be wiped out, then the holy war would be over.

It is unlikely, however, that those who want God's kingdom on earth are going to be satisfied just with a better deal for the Palestinians, or a U.S. withdrawal from Iraq. Mohammed and his friends were certainly galvanized by events in the Middle East. Samir, the "doltish Robin Hood," did go to Chechnya after all. Others left for Pakistan and Afghanistan. And Mohammed's atrocity DVDs were compiled somewhere in the Middle East.

I asked the prison imam, Ali Eddaoudi, how he assessed the link between Middle Eastern politics and European terrorism. He thought "the root of the problem" ran deeper. Sure enough, he said, the situation in the world fueled aggression. The Netherlands was an ally of the U.S. in Iraq. That couldn't be denied. And the Palestinian conflict was one good reason for Muslims to oppose the West. But "deep in their hearts," he said, most Muslims "don't have a strong connection to Iraq." The real problem, he thought, was the lack of integration in European societies. "I can distinguish between Dutch people who are anti-Islam and those who are not, but a twenty-year-old boy often can't." Instead of accepting people as citizens who have lived in the Netherlands for forty years, Dutch politicians too often "stirred things up" and encouraged hostility by blaming the immigrants for all kinds of crimes. "Every accusation hits us hard," he said. "This activates the bombs."

I asked him about the Muslim critics of Islam, such as Afshin Ellian and Ayaan Hirsi Ali. Weren't they right about the dangers of political Islam? He waved his hand, as though to dismiss the thought. Ayaan, he said, was "hypnotized by all the attention. I feel sorry for her. Ellian is more dangerous." How so? "Ellian is more thoughtful," he replied, "but he's also a Shiite. He doesn't understand anything about Moroccans, or Turks, or Sunnis." After all, he said, Shiism was really a different religion: "Ellian talks about political Islam. But I don't know anything about that. He may be right that they have that kind of thing in his native country, Iran, but he shouldn't project it onto the Netherlands."

I wondered about the difference between Shiite acts of terror and the acts of 9/11—or indeed the murder of Van Gogh—all committed by Sunnis. Were they indeed so different, despite the distinct traditions? A moment of confusion swept across Eddaoudi's handsome, bearded face. "Well, no, not really." So perhaps tradition was not so important, after all, when it came to violence in the name of faith? He brushed his hand across the surface of the Formica table, as though to wipe away a stain. After a few moments of silence, he had an answer, which was both interesting and quite disturbing: "Traditions can be like shackles. If you get rid of tradition, you still have Islam." The purity of a faith, stripped of customs and traditions, a faith to which all can be born anew, is especially attractive to young people who feel culturally and socially unhinged. "Culture," said Eddaoudi, "is made by human beings. But Islam remains."

7.

Islam remains. This appears to have been what Mohammed was hoping for when he said he prayed to Allah to preserve him from ever having to think differently. Islam was his new identity, unassailable, secure, a snug shell that would protect him from all the hostile forces around him. It gave him a sense of power, of meaning, of Truth. He would live for Islam alone. And yet even in his most ferocious writings there were unmistakable marks of Mohammed's culture, that is to say, his Dutch culture.

His angriest and perhaps most bizarre piece of writing, posted on the Internet, was entitled *To Catch a Wolf.* The title refers to an old Eskimo technique for hunting wolves. They would plant a bloody knife in the snow. The wolves, lured by the smell of blood, would approach the knife and lick the blade, cutting their tongues. They continued licking, without realizing that they were drinking their own blood, until it was too late and they had bled to death. People in the modern world, he wrote, are just like those wolves. We who live in the "democratic circus" of the West are slaves of the

"fake lollipops" of our entertainment culture, and the pernicious seductions of cafés, dance bars, and gambling halls.

The Muslim people, equally enslaved by those Western
lollipops, had reached the lowest point in their history, he
continued, but luckily rescue was at hand. The knights of
Islam would rise from . . . the Netherlands. Holland would
be the cradle of religious revolution, made possible by precisely those political liberties that Mohammed affected to
despise. He explained his weirdly paradoxical view: "Since
the Dutch political system encourages its citizens (especially
the *allochtonen,* that is, the Muslims) to take an active part
in the problems of society . . . people did indeed rise to take
on social responsibilities. Such people not only shouldered
responsibilities for the Netherlands, but for the whole world.
They will liberate the world from democratic slavery."[6]

There are echoes here of an old Dutch conceit, rooted in
a zealous type of Protestantism, the idea that Holland is the
world's moral beacon. Christians used to believe this. Just so,
it was widely believed, until not so long ago, that the Dutch
model of liberalism, multicultural tolerance, sexual permis-
siveness, and so forth, was like a ray of light shining brightly
as an example to the rest of the world that was still shrouded
in darkness. Mohammed, in a very Dutch delusion of
grandeur, expanded his youthful enthusiasm for neighborhood politics to encompass the fate of mankind. His moralism, though couched in Islamist terms, was part of this

tradition. The problem with democracy, in his view, was those sinful lollipops, the immoral pleasures of the flesh. But he had gone to an extreme that Protestants had rarely, if ever, reached. He couldn't bear the freedom to choose that attracted Ayaan Hirsi Ali. What was liberation to her was a source of unbearable frustration and confusion to him. And so he had to destroy the civilization that tormented him.

"Liberate yourself!" he admonished young Muslims, in a weird echo of 1960s Provo rhetoric. "Come out of that coffeeshop, out of that bar, out of that corner. Listen to the cry of LA ILAHA ILLA ALLAH [Forsake all others and worship only Allah]. Join the caravan of martyrs." In fact, of course, it was not at all like Provo. For the liberation preached by Mohammed was the liberation of death, of oblivion, the kind of heroic sacrifice that inspired European fascists in the 1930s.

To claim that there are similarities between Mohammed's Islamism and other kinds of extremism is not to say that they are the same. But the death wish in the name of a higher cause, a god, or a great leader is something that has appealed to confused and resentful young men through the ages and is certainly not unique to Islam. Mohammed's views on the U.S., expressed in the same document, also have a deeply European provenance, to be found in the right-wing politics of the 1930s as well as in a long left-wing tradition of anti-Americanism. "If we take the example of the mother of all democracies, America," he wrote, "and compare its social statistics (crime, violence, etc.) with those of other nations, we can only conclude that it is an utterly sick society. It is only a matter of time before the whole social order collapses into chaos."

In the muddled mind of Mohammed Bouyeri, then, ran a deep current of European anti-liberalism combined with self-righteous moralism and Islamist revolutionary fervor. This explosive mixture gave him a reason to murder the enemies who stood in the way of his vision of world salvation. The targets of his rage could be quite random, from a security guard at a local welfare office, whom Mohammed threatened with murder ("I'll rip your heart out!"), to the entire Dutch people: "The dark clouds of death gather over your country. Prepare for something you can never be prepared for. You will pay with your blood for the torture and martyrdom of our brothers and sisters."[7]

Random, but also quite specific, and there was a sexual element. Two of the three most immediate targets of Mohammed's murderous intentions were immigrants: Ayaan Hirsi Ali, a frequent subject of violent fantasies at gatherings in Mohammed's apartment, represented the civilization Mohammed wished to destroy. Ahmed Aboutaleb, the Amsterdam city councillor, was a Muslim who had allegedly turned on his brothers by working for the enemy. The third target was the populist right-wing politician, Geert Wilders, who had been trying to step into Pim Fortuyn's shiny shoes, with diminishing returns. Wilders was denounced mainly because of his alleged homosexuality. There was no basis to this allegation. Perhaps he was mixed up with Fortuyn. Or possibly his enemies were confused by the politician's trademark dyed-blond bouffant hairdo. In any case, Hirsi Ali and Aboutaleb, a thoughtful and tough-minded Social Democrat born in Morocco, were the main enemies, one an apostate, a Whore of Babylon, and the other a degraded Muslim, a *zindiq*, who was nothing but an infidel in the eyes of the followers of Takfir, and thus unworthy to live on this earth.

8.

The common view of Mohammed Bouyeri's rhetoric and deeds is to see them as deeply alien to Dutch tradition, as aspects of an exotic invasion from the mysterious and increasingly terrifying Orient. But at least one newspaper columnist recognized a similarity between the killer of Van Gogh and the fanatical vegan who murdered Pim Fortuyn. Both were "idealistic narcissists" who felt hindered in their quest for a better world, or the Truth, by loud-mouthed media celebrities.[8]

It would indeed be surprising if the general coarsening of

public rhetoric, encouraged by a constant battle to be heard in the cacophony of the mass media, and by the modern Dutch notion that "everything must be said," no matter how offensive, had not infected the habits and words of a young Dutchman of foreign extraction. Mohammed, in this sense too, was perhaps more a child of south Amsterdam than of Douar Ikhammalen.

Ali Eddaoudi, the prison imam, has no patience for the "young generation of Moroccan criminals." They are "animals," in his view, uncouth, left much too free, obsessed with money and status. Turks still send their most unruly boys back to Turkey for a while, to learn manners. Moroccan parents used to do this too, until Dutch social workers put a stop to it, thinking it was a form of "oppression." Eddaoudi would love to take some of those "animals" back to Morocco, where he would soon teach them manners by "totally humiliating them." Over there, he said, you get beaten for bad behavior. You get ostracized. You have no friends. But in Holland, it's the reverse: "If you steal, and drive around in a big car, you get status." The culture of "the old country, where few of these boys were born, isn't the problem," he concluded. "The problem is right here, in Holland."

Naturally, Mohammed Bouyeri would not regard himself as a common thug. On the contrary, he touted his brand of

Islam as the solution to the bad behavior that both he and Ali Eddaoudi condemn. Nor has he been treated as a common criminal. Judges and lawyers in criminal trials do not normally spend so much time pondering the "ideological and religious development" of the defendants. But this, too, may have something to do with an older story, much older than the current crisis among Muslims in large European cities: violent crime and revolutionary violence are not always far apart.

In November 2005, the Amsterdam police arrested a Moroccan-Dutch kid called Maik. He had twice posted violent threats against Geert Wilders on the Internet. When the police searched his house, they found homemade explosives in the basement. Maik was a street kid, like many others, with a passion for kickboxing and fireworks. He was attracted to excitement, craved action. September 11 immediately captured his imagination. His Moroccan friends at school thought Islam was cool and tough. He began to rummage around the Internet for more information. After the murder of Van Gogh, he established some kind of contact with the Hofstad Group and met Nouredine. He adopted the name Talib el-Ilm, Student of Knowledge. His hero, whose picture he used on his user profile on MSN, was his "Great leader and teacher" Mohammed Bouyeri. Maik, the kickboxer, was all of seventeen years old.

9.

November 2004 was Ramadan, the ninth month of the Islamic calendar, when all Muslims fast between sunrise and sundown. It is a time of gathering with family and friends, of prayer, and, especially toward the end of Ramadan, of charitable thoughts and good deeds.

On the evening of November 1, Mohammed received his friends at his Amsterdam apartment, which he shared with another friend named Ahmed. Jason, the half-American, was there, and Ismael, and Fahmi, and Rashid. The friends from The Hague had brought some soup. They talked about the old days, when Mohammed used to get high and tell fantastic stories. They laughed. Time passed quickly. It was past midnight when Mohammed decided to go for a walk around the Sloterplas, a pond near his apartment. He was accompanied by Rashid and Ahmed. Mohammed didn't say much, but pointed to the night sky and remarked how beautiful and peaceful it looked. They listened to Koranic prayers through their headphones attached to digital music players. Nothing much more was said.

Back at the apartment, Ahmed and Mohammed went straight to bed. It was late and they had to rise early. At 5:30 A.M. they prayed and had a light breakfast. Ahmed went back to sleep. When he woke up a few hours later, Mohammed had already left the apartment. On his bicycle, like so many other Dutch people, he was making his way to another part of Amsterdam, where he would meet another man on his bicycle. There were no surprises. He had cycled this route many times in the weeks before. He knew exactly what he was going to do.

SEVEN

In Memoriam

I have been in a total rage ever since I read in last week's paper that the Amsterdam borough of East/Watergraafsmeer refuses to build a permanent memorial to Theo van Gogh in Linnaeus Street. The borough council [Social Democrats and Greens] fears that such a memorial would lead to provocations and unrest among the Muslims living in the surrounding areas. . . . So much cowardice makes me sick.

LETTER TO HET PAROOL, JULY 13, 2005

"There certainly is a place here for a monument in memory of Theo van Gogh," says Germaine Princen, temporary chairperson of the East/Watergraafsmeer council. . . . Princen believes that unrest in the neighborhood should not be a reason to abandon the idea of a monument. A mural commemorating the murder has already been defaced twice.

NRC HANDELSBLAD, JULY 12, 2005

And so the bickering went on. Should a memorial be built on Linnaeus Street, on the spot of the murder, or in the neighboring park, or perhaps in the center of

Amsterdam, or maybe not at all? And what kind of monument should it be? *Het Parool,* a newspaper founded by the Dutch resistance under Nazi occupation, invited its readers to come up with ideas for the most appropriate memorial: a two-meters-high cigarette, suggested one reader, from which puffs of smoke would emerge at regular intervals; a sculpture of a great happy pig, said another, on whose pink flanks people could write their opinions. Many liked the idea of a sculpture in the form of a giant cactus—a cactus, in the words of one reader, employing the quaintly old-fashioned jargon of postwar novels about war heroes, "that was just as big and strong as Theo, as a beacon of prickly power, as an inspiration to stand tall, proud and undaunted."

The cactus had become something of a trademark for Van Gogh. He would always end his television talk shows by kissing one, after inviting his guests to do the same. One of his guests, Roman Polanski, refused. Van Gogh, who idolized Polanski, said he loved kissing cacti. Polanski replied that everyone has to be good at something.

Erecting monuments to their own bravery and suffering during World War II had become so prevalent a Dutch practice in the late 1940s and early '50s that people spoke of a "monument rain." The largest and most famous one, a kind of fluted stone phallus with reliefs all around of suffering Dutch humanity in chains, is the National Monument on Dam Square, opposite the royal palace in Amsterdam. The

Queen lays a wreath there every year to remember World War II—not the Holocaust, which was hardly an issue in the 1950s, but the suffering of the Dutch people under German occupation. It is where the nation feels most sorry for itself. (It is also where the world's young gathered in the 1960s and '70s to strum guitars, make out in their sleeping bags, and smoke dope.)

One of the readers of *Het Parool* took the view that the National Monument should make way for a cactus monument that would be just as large and imposing. In the eyes of such people, Van Gogh had finally become what he had aspired to be: the symbol of Dutch resistance, the national hero who stood tall, a freedom fighter who did his uncle and grandfather proud. The cactus idea won. A decision was made by the borough council of East/Watergraafsmeer to erect the stone cactus in the park where Mohammed Bouyeri was arrested, not far from the place where he killed Van Gogh.

The bickering did not stop with the monument, however. Just as contentious was the first anniversary of the murder, to be commemorated in Linnaeus Street. Job Cohen, the mayor, would speak, and so would the prime minister, Jan Peter Balkenende. This was enough reason for the Friends of Theo to stay away. "We have not been invited," Theodor Holman sniffed in his weekly column for *Het Parool,* and surely Cohen "must have" regarded Theo as an anti-Semite—"which he wasn't."

And so, intoned Theo's best Friend: "Fuck off, Job Cohen! We know you always hated Theo. . . .

> *"Shut down those filthy mosques, goddamn it, where they really preach anti-Semitism and want to kill you and my kind. Throw those fucking fundamentalists out of the country! Or, better still, sew the butchers up in bags and drop them into the sea!*
>
> *"That's the way to remember Theo!"*[1]

The language, as usual with Holman, was extreme, and the sentiments deeply unpleasant. Yet it is worth quoting because the tone was not unique. I hesitate to attach national characteristics to this particular air of aggrieved self-righteousness, but Holman's outburst, in a perfectly respectable Amsterdam daily, expressed something that is not uncommon in Holland today: offensiveness projected as a sign of sincerity, the venting of rage as a mark of moral honesty. Theo van Gogh himself, of course, had done much to set this tone.

As it happened, the memorial ceremony in Linnaeus Street was a calm and dignified occasion. There were flowers, a teddy bear, messages of grief, and a large pale green cactus, sticking up from the bicycle path like a hairy cucumber. The one bit of discord was a placard held up by a woman that read: "Balkenende, you're here one year too late." But after the prime minister went over to have a quiet word with her, she raised her thumb and praised him for being such a fine fellow. She had only been upset, she said, because he had visited vandalized Moroccan schools after Theo's murder. Why, she asked him, did he have to pay so much attention to "those Moroccans"? After all, she said with tears in her eyes, he was the "Dutch prime minister."

The crowd was relatively small, a few hundred people at most. Followers of Pim Fortuyn wore T-shirts with portraits of Van Gogh and their own hero fraternally side by side, as freedom fighters. Balkenende spoke about the importance of the rule of law. The murder, he said, was an attack on "everything we hold dear in the Netherlands." Cohen, too, appealed to reason: "We must be free to believe what we want, free to say what we think, and free to go where we wish, without fear."

The crowd began to disperse. It was just another office day. Of the dignitaries, only the Amsterdam council member, Ahmed Aboutaleb, lingered. He explained to reporters, in his faint Moroccan accent, that he was there in support of the constitution, which had been brutally assaulted by the murder of Van Gogh. Candles were lit by one or two of the Fortuyn followers. A gust of wind caught the flames and the prickly cactus was swiftly reduced to a pile of ashes.

There was one more commemoration that day, in the Arena Hotel in Amsterdam. This time, Theo's family and

Friends did turn up, even though Job Cohen spoke once again, about freedom and tolerance and the need to face life without fear. Theo's father, Johan, thanked people for their support, and a discussion followed, which was largely an opportunity to express goodwill and liberal sentiments. Oh, for "a brilliant debater like Theo van Gogh," lamented one observer. How deplorable that "most people there were well educated and susceptible to reason." Only Holman did not disappoint. "Do you really think Theo would have been happy with this?" he roared. "He would have loathed it! Can I say that I read the Koran and thought it was a fucking rotten book? Only at the risk of my life."

The fighting over Theo van Gogh's remembrance was unseemly, but not untypical of a country with a long tradition of religious strife. Memory, especially in ceremonies for the dead, is not about debate, but about shared emotion, often cast in a religious or quasi-religious form. The Netherlands, like the rest of western Europe, may have become a largely secular society in recent decades, but the habits of faith die hard. Preaching still comes naturally to the Dutch, as does the venting of moralizing emotion—that sense of being "in a total rage." Emotion, one year after Theo's murder, had largely lifted the victim out of the history of actual events and elevated him to an almost mythical status as a martyr for the pure and absolute truth.

It is always easier, particularly in what was once a deeply

religious country, to erect memorials and deliver sermons than to look the angel of history directly in the face. The way people remembered Theo van Gogh was marked by a surfeit not of reason but of sentimentality. It is a common feature of the secular age, these outbursts of displaced religiosity, often expressed at the funerals of media celebrities: Princess Diana, Pope John Paul II, Pim Fortuyn, Theo van Gogh. The tearful farewells to people we never knew have replaced the established forms of organized faith, which used to absorb, in the shape of confessions or common prayer, more personal anxieties and discontents. Collective sentimentality is the easiest way to deal with matters we would rather not face head-on. This is evident in many painful memories, including those of the darkest past, that still haunt the Dutch, perhaps even more than other Europeans. If Clio is the muse of history, the ghostly presence of Anne Frank has hovered over the collective memory of Nazi occupation.

2.

The Amsterdam apartment where Anne Frank began her diary before going into hiding from the Nazis has been restored to the style of the 1930s to create a refuge for persecuted writers. . . . Using photographs from the family archive and a

letter from Anne Frank describing the apartment, a team of
experts worked for months to remove modern fixtures and
decorate and furnish the residence in the same style it was
left in by the family. A carpenter reconstructed the writing
table at which the 13-year-old probably started her diary in
June 1942, weeks before disappearing into the secret annex of
a canal-side warehouse to hide during German occupation of
the Netherlands. . . .

   The first resident of the apartment at Merwedeplein in
southern Amsterdam is Algerian novelist and poet el-Mahdi
Acherchour, 32, who is working on a new novel.

REUTERS, OCTOBER 28, 2005

I was struck by this news item, not because I begrudged a persecuted writer his refuge in Amsterdam. Offering an Algerian, or any other writer, a place to work in freedom and peace is a good and noble undertaking. But the exact re-creation of Anne Frank's old family apartment, so that a writer can dwell in her ghostly presence, is morbid and in-deed sentimental—as though the past could be relived by re-creating its settings, as though there is anything to be learned, apart from one or two things about interior deco-ration, by restoring the period fixtures of Anne Frank's liv-ing room. Sometimes it is better to let the past be.

Yet I, too, found it hard to forget the past during the

summer months I spent in Amsterdam. Friends had lent me their house in the oldest part of the city. It stands on a narrow street that once ran through a medieval nunnery. The area, now part of the most famous red-light district in Europe, is nothing if not cosmopolitan. On one corner of the street is a Thai massage parlor, on the other a brothel with three Brazilian transvestites, one of whom advertised his particular assets in a photograph of a large brown penis drooping above a gartered leg.

The virtually naked "window prostitutes," from all the poor countries in the world, pose in their dimly lit rooms along the canal, in old houses decorated with gracefully carved seventeenth- and eighteenth-century gables and neon signs offering live sex shows. It is easier in that part of town to buy a large electric dildo than a newspaper. Drunken Englishmen in T-shirts and razor haircuts slouch past the windows in groups, sniggering and pointing at the girls from Guatemala or Ukraine. Turkish men with sad mustaches negotiate prices with their hands, while black men from Suriname do drug deals under the trees by the bridge. Bewildered groups of Chinese tourists are ushered into the sex shows by Dutch hawkers, who offer "fucky fucky, sucky sucky" while making obscene gestures with their tongues. Sex shops are stacked with magazines and DVDs catering to fantasies of every conceivable taste. Inflatable dolls with wide-open mouths, rhino whips, leather masks, penis rings, and large photos of blowjobs and anal penetrations are openly on display.

A stench of beer, marijuana, rotting garbage, and piss hangs like vapor over the historic canals. A friend of mine once admonished a couple of Moroccan youths for urinating against the wooden door of a fine seventeenth-century townhouse. Why not use the canal, he suggested. For an instant, they were taken by surprise, but then told him in perfect Amsterdam accents to "mind your own business, you fucking Jew!"

Perhaps Western civilization, with the Amsterdam red-light district as its fetid symbol, does have something to answer for. Maybe these streets are typical of a society without modesty, morally unhinged. Such a naked display of man's animal instincts could be seen as a form of barbarism. For people whose faith is predicated on modesty and whose code of honor prohibits any display of female sexuality, every single window along that Amsterdam canal is an intolerable provocation. You might say that nobody asked those people to live in Amsterdam. But they were encouraged to come and work there, and their children were born there. They *are* there, whether one likes it or not, and the Dutch prime minister is their prime minister too.

The red-light district on one side of my street became wearisome in its relentness exploitation of human lust.

Though intrigued by its more colorful denizens, I grew tired of it and spent more time on the other side of the street, which leads to a large square, the Nieuwmarkt, one of the oldest in Amsterdam, where the open-air cafés face a scene that sometimes filled me with a far greater melancholy than the crassest sex emporium. On the far side of the Nieuwmarkt is an old section of the city whose narrow, densely populated streets were once lined with higgledy-piggledy row houses, some dating back to the early seventeenth century. Almost all those houses are gone now, replaced by buildings of the 1980s, whose slick white modernity makes them stand out in the historic heart of Amsterdam. It used to be known as the *jodenhoek*, Jews' corner.

During the war a barbed wire fence separated one side of the square from the *jodenhoek*. Amsterdam never actually had a ghetto, unlike Warsaw, even though the Germans had made plans for one at the beginning of the war. After much consideration, the idea was abandoned because it would have caused too much inconvenience to gentiles, who would have had to move out of the area. But the Nazi authorities did force more and more Jews, many of them from the provinces, to move into three overcrowded Amsterdam neighborhoods, one of which was the *jodenhoek*.

This part of the city, with its seventeenth-century Portuguese and German synagogues and its lively street markets, had long been populated by Jews, most of them poor. Rembrandt lived there too, however, and picked the models for his biblical paintings from the streets around his studio. Before the German occupation more than eighty thousand Jews resided in Amsterdam. By the end of the war about five thousand had survived.

After the last cattle train to "the east" had left in 1943, the *jodenhoek* was like a ghost town. The houses, emptied of their inhabitants, had been looted for wood to stoke the fires of Amsterdammers during the icy "hunger winter" of 1944–45. And so for three decades after the war they remained, gutted and increasingly falling apart, often with the Jewish family names of abandoned shops still faintly showing on crumbling walls. Many of the houses were later demolished, leaving large gaps filled with rubbish. People preferred not to think about the reasons for this urban ruination. The remains of a human catastrophe were simply left to rot. The few houses that were still there in the 1970s were taken over by young squatters, until, finally, around 1974, the last remnants of the *jodenhoek* were swept away to build an underground railway station and a new opera house.

But first the squatters had to be removed from their improvised homes. What followed was a kind of grotesque reenactment of the historic drama. Not that the Dutch police, using batons and waterhoses to flush out the squatters, had anything in common with the Nazis, or that the squatters were destined to be murdered. It was just that the spectacle of uniformed men dragging people from their homes, while we watched the action behind fortified barriers, conjured up images I had only seen in blurry photographs taken on that very spot three decades before.

Before remembering the Holocaust, in memorials and textbooks, became an almost universal Western ritual in the late 1960s, only two monuments in the *jodenhoek* stood as reminders of what happened there. One, a relief in white stone, was erected in 1950. It is called the monument of "Jewish Gratitude"—gratitude to the Dutch people who stood by the Jewish victims. The other, built two years later, is a sculpture of a burly workingman, with his head held high, and his meaty arms and large proletarian fists spread in a gesture of angry defiance. The Dockworker is a monument to the two-day "February Strike" of 1941, when Amsterdam stopped working in protest against the deportation of 425 Jewish men to a concentration camp. The men had been brutally rounded up in plain sight of many gentiles shopping at the popular Sunday market. Word spread quickly: city cleaners refused to collect garbage, mail was not delivered, trams stopped running, and the port of Amsterdam was silent for forty-eight hours.

This show of solidarity, unique in Europe, and largely responsible for the high reputation of Holland among Jews, is certainly worth remembering, but it is also misleading. Though not exactly mythical—it really happened, after all— the February Strike was a convenient symbol to shield people from more painful memories, of having stood by and watched and done nothing. Others, to be sure, had risked their lives, and those of their families, to hide Jews. But this great story of bravery, for a time, was used to mask a larger history of indifference, cowardice, and in some cases active complicity.

I would occasionally drink coffee on Saturday mornings at a busy café on the Nieuwmarkt with a distinguished Dutch historian named Geert Mak. Mak had annoyed the Friends of Theo and other combatants in the war against radical Islam by taking a more relativistic view of the problem. A stocky man with a woolly thatch of silvery curls, Mak projects the voice of a friendly, liberal-minded small-town history teacher. He often spoke to me about the old Left, whose politics he himself largely shared; about the affronted turn of some progressives against Muslim immigrants; and about their nostalgia for "a classical Holland of the 1950s"—the Holland of Johan Huizinga, *satisfait,* enlightened, middle-of-the-road, bourgeois. Mak, in a way, personifies these solid virtues. His books on Dutch history are all bestsellers. They provide a comforting historical narrative for a people that feels deprived of a historical identity. Like the sentimentality at celebrity funerals, this is not a uniquely Dutch phenomenon either. National histories have become popular everywhere in a world beset by corporate uniformity.

Despite the wild reputation of Amsterdam, Mak says, Holland never had a truly metropolitan culture. Learning to live with large numbers of immigrants is "going to be a difficult and painful process," and people will just "have to get used to it." After all, hadn't the Jews in nineteenth-century Amsterdam been integrated quite successfully by enlightened policies? Hadn't it been a good thing to subsidize schools for the Jewish poor, on condition that they be taught in Dutch and not Yiddish? The same kind of thing could work again. But this process would not be helped by anti-Muslim hysteria. Mak disapproves of Ayaan Hirsi Ali's "Jeanne d'Arc–like antics." Van Gogh, in his view, was a "tragic Dutchman" who had been "tricked" into making the film that cost him his life. The problem, he maintains, is not Islam, or religion as such. It is more sociological. What we are witnessing is nothing new. Just the usual tensions that occur when uprooted rural people start new lives in the metropolis.

Soon after Van Gogh's violent death, Mak published two pamphlets attacking what he saw as the dangerous and hysterical intolerance of Muslims in the Dutch media and among politicians. As Holland's most popular historian, he saw it as his role to bring common sense to the national debate. By and large, he succeeded, but even Mak, the paragon of Huizinga's virtues, could not escape entirely from the ghost of Anne Frank, from the Dutch habit of filtering the present through guilty memories of what happened in the *jodenhoek*. In one of his pamphlets he compared the narrative technique of Hirsi Ali's film *Submission* to the viciously anti-Semitic Nazi propaganda film *The Eternal Jew.*

In a very narrow technical sense—the selective use of damning quotations, for instance—he may have had a point, but the comparison struck a false note. Hirsi Ali spoke out against oppression, not for it. The exclusion of Muslims, or any other group, is not part of her program. And yet to reach for examples from the Holocaust, or the Jewish diaspora, has become a natural reflex when the question of ethnic or religious minorities comes up. It is a moral yardstick, yet at the same time an evasion. To be reminded of past crimes, of negligence or complicity, is never a bad thing. But it can confuse the issues at hand, or worse, bring all discussion to a halt by tarring opponents with the brush of mass murder. This issue is not the Holocaust, but the question of how to stop future Mohammed Bouyeris from becoming violent enemies of the country in which they grew up—how to make those boys pissing on the seventeenth-century door feel that this is their home too.

Time *magazine's selection of Job Cohen as one of the European heroes in 2005 has left deep wounds in the ranks of his enemies . . . on the Pim Fortuyn Forum website we find such statements as: "Unbelievable that such a traitor is seen as a hero in the U.S.!" or "Cohen is a Jewish name and there are many Cohens in the U.S. as well," or "Cohen is partly responsible for the reason Van Gogh was murdered."* FRITS ABRAHAMS, COLUMNIST FOR *NRC HANDELSBLAD,* OCTOBER 10, 2005

Dear Mr. Cohen,

You made a great and fundamental mistake when you stated that Muslim minorities in the Netherlands could be integrated through their religion. Since your Cleveringa Lecture in 2002 more and more people have pointed out your error, yet you stick to your mistaken view. AYAAN HIRSI ALI, OPEN LETTER TO JOB COHEN, MARCH 8, 2004

The annual Cleveringa Lecture, delivered at Leiden University on the twenty-sixth of November, is named after a brave man who never raised his voice or gave deliberate offense. He was a hero because he was decent, and said the right thing at a time when decency could have severe consequences.

The exclusion of one section of Dutch citizens under German occupation began in 1940 when civil servants were ordered to sign forms declaring whether they were "Aryans" or Jews. Most people did, often without quite realizing the implications. Then, soon after, the Germans announced that Jews would be removed from public office. At Leiden University, three distinguished academics, Meijers, David, and Gans, were dismissed. Professor Eduard Meijers was one of the most famous legal scholars of his generation, responsible for the modern civil code.

These measures were accepted, more or less grudgingly, by most Dutch authorities, but not by the dean of the law faculty in Leyden, Professor Rudolph Cleveringa. On November 26, 1940, he decided to speak in protest to the faculty and students. He chose the time normally reserved for Meijers's lectures, and began by reading aloud, verbatim, the letter ordering his colleague's dismissal. The cold pen-pusher's language was incriminating enough. Instead of addressing the obscenity of political racism directly, Cleveringa went on to praise his colleague as "a man of light" whom "a power that can rest on nothing but itself" was casting aside. Then he spoke the famous words which still resonate: "It is this Dutchman, this noble and true son of our people, this human being, this father for his students, this scholar, whom the hostile alien that rules over us today is 'dismissing from his job.'"

Job Cohen, in his Cleveringa Lecture of 2002, continued the story: "In the great auditorium on that memorable November morning in 1940 sat a young Jewish law student. Cleveringa's words were like balsam to her doubting soul. She had the feeling, at that moment, that 'our soundless thoughts and moods were being transmitted through one and all in a way that everyone could precisely recognize.' And especially that one feeling, more powerful than all others: 'I belong!' "

Cleveringa knew what he was doing. He had already packed his bags. The following day the students went on strike in protest against the dismissals, and Cleveringa was arrested. The student mentioned by Cohen was his own mother. Speaking for her, and for himself, a liberal, assimilated Jew, Cohen hailed the tolerance of Dutch society, and the way people of all races and creeds had found a home there. But then, the shock of 9/11, the murder of Pim Fortuyn, and the "hardening" of attitudes toward immigrants had changed the social climate. He wondered: "Do 'they' still belong as much as they did before 11 September 2001? Many Dutch citizens of foreign origin must have thought to themselves in the last few years: Is this really Holland? Do I still belong? Am I not a stranger in my own country?"

Drawing the link between his own mother's experience as a Jew under Nazi occupation and Muslim immigrants today was bound to disturb people. How could the two be equated? Wasn't this an example of the sentimental use of Holocaust memories where they didn't apply? I actually think not. Cohen wasn't talking about genocide, but about belonging. There was no question, of course, that Cohen's mother, and Professor Meijers, felt that they belonged. Many young Muslims born and bred in Europe feel that they don't. The question is why.

There was much in Cohen's lecture about the rule of law, about norms and values, the erosion of organized faith, the problems of multiculturalism and global capitalism, but he kept returning to that basic question: how to make people feel at home in a modern, secular, liberal society in which many customs and values, and indeed collective memories, clash with their own? Cohen's answer is that this shouldn't matter, as long as people do not break the law. It is, in any case, not as clear as it was in Huizinga's day what it is to be Dutch (or French, or German). Quoting Geert Mak, Cohen suggested that "a new adhesive" was needed to "glue society together." Without making it entirely clear what this glue should be, Cohen stressed the importance of mutual respect. This means, in his view, that we should tolerate opinions and habits even if we do not share them, or even approve of them. We tolerate the fact that women are not allowed to become members of an ultra-Calvinist political party. Just so, we have to "tolerate certain groups of orthodox Muslims who consciously discriminate against their women."

Cohen went further. Why not revive the Dutch idea of the pillar? Dutch citizens used to organize their lives through their religious affiliations. Perhaps Muslims should be encouraged to do the same. Then he spoke the sentence that most upset his critics: "The easiest way to integrate these new immigrants might be through their faith. For that is just about the only anchor they have when they enter Dutch society in the twenty-first century." This was seen as rank appeasement; a reason for Theo van Gogh to compare Cohen to a Nazi collaborator.

Ayaan Hirsi Ali believes that Cohen is "fighting demons from the past," that "true Islam" is irreconcilable with a secular, liberal state, that Muslims, unlike Jews in the 1930s, are not hated in Europe today, but that they, the Muslims, hate secular, liberal Europe. The idea that "true Muslims" can be integrated through the mosque, she says, is to make the same naive mistake as the U.S. government, which supported the Taliban against the Soviet Union, only to see the believers bite back and destroy the Twin Towers. A true Muslim, she argues, believes that a conspiracy of Jews is running the world; a true Muslim thinks democracy is sinful, and that only God's laws must be obeyed; a true Muslim, in short, is the enemy of all freedom-loving heirs of the Enlightenment, and the fact that Cohen fails to see this shows how blinded he is by those historic demons that once threatened the life of his mother.

If all true Muslims were political revolutionaries, Ayaan Hirsi Ali would doubtless be right. But since this is not the case, even among orthodox Muslims, Cohen deserves the benefit of the doubt. If Islam as such were a threat to democracy, then all Muslims are threats. It is precisely to avoid this notion of Kulturkampf, or "clash of civilizations," that Cohen wants to reach an accommodation with the Muslims in his city. It is easy, as Hirsi Ali does, to find hateful examples on websites and in radical sermons of violent anti-Semitism and loathing of Western civilization. And it's true that discrimination of Muslim women by their own fathers and brothers causes much suffering, but it is hard to see how an official attack on the Muslim faith would help to solve this problem. The revolutionaries are no longer open to compromise, and apart from giving protection to young women who are subject to male violence, there is little the government can do to change the habits of conservative patriarchs. Attacking religion cannot be the answer, for the real threat to a mixed society will come when the mainstream of non-revolutionary Muslims has lost all hope of feeling at home.

4.

On average, Moroccan youths have 30% less chance of finding apprentice jobs than their autochthonous contemporaries. In the building trade their chances are actually three times less. There is a strong demand only in the bar and restaurant business. This is the conclusion of a research project by Utrecht University, commissioned by the Green/Left Party.

VOLKSKRANT, AUGUST 27, 2005

On July 5 councillor Ahmed Aboutaleb spoke with Islamic schools in Amsterdam because of a recent municipal report which showed that a disproportionate number of Muslim, and particularly Moroccan, youths had turned against Western society. . . . Aboutaleb mentioned that "the pupils feel disadvantaged. Teachers try to give their own opinions instead of stimulating a dialogue." COLUMN IN HET PAROOL, JULY 30, 2005

Ahmed Aboutaleb was born in the Rif mountains of Morocco in 1961, as the son of a village imam. In 1976 his mother took him and his brothers to the Netherlands. After learning Dutch and completing his education in telecommunications, he worked as a radio reporter, and later as chairman of Forum, the multicultural organization. He is a member of the Social Democrats. His current job, Amsterdam councillor, came as a surprise. In 2002, his predecessor, Rob Oudkerk, also a Social Democrat, made a serious error. At the end of a public meeting, thinking the microphone was switched off, Oudkerk, whose grandfather served on the Jewish Council under Nazi occupation, leaned over to Job Cohen and whispered something about "those fucking Moroccans" (*kutmarokkanen*). In 2004, he was succeeded by Ahmed Aboutaleb.

Aboutaleb, whose portfolio includes youth affairs, education, integration, and urban policy, has been called worse things than a fucking Moroccan. Once, in a television talk show, he was accused by a history teacher of Moroccan descent of being an NSBer, a Nazi collaborator. It was a very strange thing for one Berber to say to another, even if "NSBer" has become a generic term of abuse. Perhaps the use of this historical parallel was a sign, on the side of the accuser, of integration into Dutch society. Aboutaleb did not see it that way and threatened to sue.

What does it mean, anyway, for a highly respected Amsterdam councillor to be a "collaborator"? Collaborator with what? A trawl through Dutch websites of various political shades reveals how Aboutaleb gets it from all sides. The history teacher mentioned above, named Abdelhakim Chouaati, writes for elqalem.nl, a website for young Moroccans which pays respectful attention to all kinds of anti-

Semitic conspiracy theories. In the chatrooms of elqalem.nl, Aboutaleb is frequently called a traitor, a kiss-ass, a "subsidy whore," or a Bounty, after a famous coconut-filled chocolate bar—brown on the outside, white on the inside.

Mohammed Bouyeri, in his death threat to Aboutaleb, addressed him as a heretic, or *zindiq*, which makes him an enemy of Islam destined for execution. Aboutaleb's sin, for Mohammed, and for Abdelhakim too, is precisely his success as a Dutch citizen. To take part in government, to promote integration, to speak out against the violent prejudices of religious zealots, is enough to make him a heretic, an enemy, a traitor. But, then, trawling a little farther through the byways of cyberspace, I found a Dutch neo-Nazi website, Stormfront.org, which denounces Aboutaleb as a slave to the worldwide Jewish conspiracy, led by "the arch Zionist Cohen." These are the rancid margins, of course, where Islamist extremists and white supremacists find one another in a peculiar meeting of minds. But even in the mainstream of society, the Amsterdam councillor often cuts a lonely figure.

When twenty thousand people gathered on Dam Square on the day of Van Gogh's murder to demonstrate their anger, Aboutaleb was one of only a handful of Muslims. This was a disappointment to him. "Even though they might have found Van Gogh an asshole," he says, "they should have been there to defend the rule of law." He could barely contain his own rage. In a speech to fellow Muslims, delivered in an Amsterdam mosque (Aboutaleb is a pious man), he said that tolerance was not a one-way street. Amsterdam was a city of freedom and diversity, and "those who can't share those values had better draw their own conclusions and leave."[2] This robust attitude was much applauded among the "natives," but did nothing to burnish his reputation among the immigrants.

He was everywhere in those volatile and dangerous days after the murder, trying to douse the flames of hatred and fear—in mosques, youth centers, schools. Muslims, he pleaded with the believers, "must not allow their faith to be hijacked by fanatics." But he felt abandoned by the politicians, including the prime minister. "So often," he lamented, "I stood alone in those halls. Where were all the ministers and cabinet secretaries?"[3]

Trying to build bridges can be a bitter task. By trying to accommodate disparate communities with very different demands, an official like Aboutaleb risks losing sympathy on all sides. The same man who pleaded, against all the trends of modern society, for separate swimming lessons for girls and boys, also told Muslims who couldn't abide the open society to pack their bags and leave. He even tried to plug young Muslims into the Dutch collective memory. On May 4, 2003, the national day of remembrance, Moroccan kids had outraged the natives by playing soccer with wreaths laid in honor to the war dead. So on the fourth of May 2005, Aboutaleb took a group of schoolchildren to Auschwitz.

I first saw Aboutaleb at my usual café on the Nieuwmarkt. He was reading the papers, surrounded by bodyguards. Like Ayaan Hirsi Ali, he needed full-time protection. I made an appointment to see him at the city hall, in the middle of the former *jodenhoek*. A neat, compact figure in steel-rimmed spectacles, Aboutaleb spoke about religion in the brisk and measured manner of a man who has answered the same questions many times. Religion, to him, is a private affair, in which the state has no business interfering, or the other way round. Nor is he keen on political parties organized on the basis of faith or ethnicity. The main problem, he continued, was "the matter of priorities, the fact that many Muslims find the law less important than an insult to the Prophet."

But, he said, there were generational distinctions. The first generation is barely literate. For them "religion is a matter of hearsay couched in cultural patterns. They pray five times a day, they wear beards. Jihad, for them, is not so much armed struggle as simply being a pious Muslim." The young have a different handicap, he explained. "They must consume religion in a strange language. The Koran is a complicated text, difficult to interpret, both in sociological and linguistic terms. So it makes me laugh when a kid like

Mohammed B. thinks he can derive enough knowledge from the Koran in English and Dutch to think it is his duty to gun a person down."

Even though religion is his own business, Aboutaleb sees no reason why he shouldn't be openly critical of it. What prompted the history teacher's particular ire was a famous episode involving Aboutaleb and a book compiled in the thirteenth century. One day, in the radical Tawheed Mosque, where Mohammed Bouyeri used to pray, a book was spotted, entitled *Fatwas on Women,* by the Sunni scholar Ibn Taymiyah (1263–1328). The book, sold at the mosque, included decrees about the duty of men to beat their women with rods if they should be caught telling a lie. But this was not the worst. It also contained a passage about homosexuals who should be dropped to their deaths from five-story towers. Aboutaleb wrote a letter to the mosque warning that such inflammatory material was "contrary to the letter and spirit of the law." The mosque protested that there was nothing wrong with the book, but it was withdrawn nonetheless.

Ahmed Aboutaleb is tired of the Tawheed Mosque and its zealots. He is angry at the ignorant and violent youths who, in the name of Allah and his Prophet, make it so much harder for peaceful Muslims to become accepted citizens in a European democracy, and to feel at home there, without drawing undue attention to themselves, like the Jews who came before them. And so, Ahmed Aboutaleb, councillor, bridge builder, and good Muslim, is called a Bounty, a *zindiq*, and a traitor, who deserves nothing less than death.

5.

They are called Ryan Babel, Urby Emanuelson, Prince Rajkomar, Dwight Tiendalli, Kenneth Vermeer and Gianni Zuiverloon, and are of Surinamese descent. Or they have Antillean blood and bear such names as Kemy Agustien and Hedwiges Maduro.

Quincy Owusu Abeyie's parents come from Ghana, and Ibrahim Afellay could choose to play either for Morocco or Holland. Then there are the refugees, Collins John (Liberia) and Haris Medunjanin (Bosnia).

When the national team coach, Foppe de Haan, surveys his players in "Orange Under-20," he sees "a cross section of the Dutch population." VOLKSKRANT, JUNE 10, 2005

The day I went to see the history teacher Abdelhakim Chouaati in Rotterdam was the occasion for a major postwar national ritual: Holland was playing Germany in a soccer match. These games are often more than games. Especially when a World or European Cup is contested, they are a ceremonial reenactment of World War II. Germany must be defeated. No doubt the Poles feel the same way, and even the English, although they never suffered under German occupation. This is partly a result of changing political mores. Open displays of patriotism have become a taboo in post–World War II Europe, except on the soccer field. It is as if there, and only there, all the forbidden tribal sentiments are allowed to be vented in massive displays of flag waving, anthem singing, and primitive warrior worship. When Holland plays Germany, thousands of men, women, and children don their royalist orange uniforms to do battle with the traditional foe, the enemy whose very existence allows the Dutch to adopt a self-regarding national identity: the liberal, open, tolerant, free-spirited Dutch, versus the mechanical, disciplined, authoritarian Teutons. When Holland beat Germany in the European Cup finals in 1988, more people came out to celebrate in the streets of Amsterdam than on the day of liberation in 1945.

Abdelhakim, sitting in a café near the central railway station, gazed at the supporters in their orange suits, orange scarves, and orange hats, sometimes adorned with plastic replicas of clogs, or windmills, or great yellow cheeses, with an air of supreme indifference, like a bored Western tourist watching an interminable display of folk dancing in some Third World country. The orange men, almost all white, and many on the wrong side of thirty, danced jigs on the station square while breaking into snatches of the national anthem, or an old children's song celebrating Dutch valor in the face of seventeenth-century Spanish rule.

Since national history has been more or less wiped off the Dutch history curriculum, many children would not know much, if anything, about the war of independence against the Spanish crown. Songs celebrating it are now as quaint as those clogs and windmills, sported as national badges on top of the supporters' hats, clichés of a legendary past, recycled for soccer matches and the tourist trade. They certainly hold no attraction for Abdelhakim.

But I was curious to know what he, as a teacher of the subject, made of Dutch history. So I asked him about his education in a small Calvinist town near Rotterdam, where his father had found work in a steel factory. Abdelhakim, a slim man in his twenties, looked at me askance, past his aquiline nose, a look that reminded me of radical Maoists or Trotskyists in my student days, arrogant and defensive at the same time. It was a look that said: All people who haven't seen the light are idiots, barely worth speaking to, but idiots are dangerous, so one has to be vigilant, and be prepared to combat idiocy at every turn.

Dutch history? Abdelhakim shrugged. "Just a lot of self-congratulatory guff. A lot of whining about the Jews. Well, Muslims didn't invent the gas chambers. So why did the Jews have to be dumped in Palestine?" His answer was a sad reflection of how much history had become narrowed down to only one or two themes. Anne Frank's shadow falls heavily on the school curriculum too. But I felt we were getting off the subject a little too fast, so I asked him what children were taught about history in his school.

"Lies," he said, one eye peering at me intently. "All lies. Darwinism, for example. They don't say anything about creationism. They're too scared to attribute evolution to God." He gave a barely perceptible snort of derision. "Perhaps they're afraid of looking too much like Muslims."

In fact, Abdelhakim did not seem very interested in history, certainly not in Dutch history, which he found trivial. "I only teach history to make money," he said. What did interest him were conspiracies. His theories were conventional enough, in certain circles: 9/11 was a Jewish plot. Why else did four thousand Jews in New York stay home that day? More surprising to me was his view that the first landing on the moon was faked by CIA agents in Hollywood. It never happened, he maintained. The filmed images were made by Stanley Kubrick, the famous Jewish director. The agents were later murdered to erase the evidence of this great fraud.

Abdelhakim does not come from a religious family. When he relaxed a bit, he said that his parents, both moderate people, were worried about him. He was "a bit of a black sheep," who "went my own way." None of his sisters wears a headscarf. His politics are a mixture of Third World resentments— "The West thinks it can do anything it likes in the world, and it's all about making money"—and religious conservatism—his anti-Darwinist views, his puritanical attitudes to sex. He said he would marry an Arab woman and bring his children up as strict Muslims.

I wanted to know how he felt about being Dutch. How did he fit in? Nationality, he said, meant nothing to him. Islam is all that matters. He is a Muslim living in Holland. What about the Dutch laws? Was there any tension between the secular constitution and the Shariah? No problem, he said. He could abide by the constitution. He obeys the laws. He stops at a red light. It is true that the Shariah, "being divine, is outside time, and thus for all time." But, he observed, "90 percent of Dutch law matches the Shariah." As far as the remaining 10 percent is concerned, Islamic criminal law is stricter. "Pedophiles get the death penalty under Shariah. In Holland they get their own association." He found this rather amusing. His sneer softened into a mocking smile.

There can be no doubt: Abdelhakim is an uncompromising believer. He says so himself. That is why his parents are worried about him. But this in itself does not make him unusual. In the sense that the Koran is believed to consist of God's own words, most Muslims are fundamentalists. But some are prepared to live peacefully in secular societies, and some are not. Abdelhakim counts himself among the former. Being a fundamentalist does not make him a revolutionary.

As long as he is allowed to practice his religion, he says, he is happy to live in Holland, certainly happier than he would be anywhere in the Middle East. Indeed, he thinks Muslims "have a very good life here." He does not condone killing anybody for his beliefs, or the lack of them. "We are still guests here. The majority is not Muslim and the Shariah can only be introduced if the majority wants it." He would certainly welcome it if everyone shared his faith, but then so would most Christians.

In some ways, Abdelhakim may be more Dutch than he thinks. His idea of helping young Muslim delinquents mend their ways through faith is what Christians would favor too. The idea of using the mosque to keep angry young men on the straight and narrow is conservative, but hardly alien to a society that rested on religious "pillars" until a few decades ago. Abdelhakim did not vote himself, he said, because of his orthodox faith, but it came as no great surprise to me when he mentioned the names of conservative Christian Democrats as the politicians he most admired. In an eccentric way, Abdelhakim is spiritually akin to an older, more orthodox Dutch society, which was mostly swept away by the cultural tide of the 1960s.

This is not to say that there is nothing disturbing about him. The anti-Semitism is vile. And I'm not sure he would be so tolerant of infidels if he lived in a society under Shariah law. But he did not strike me as a dangerous man. Not yet. The fact that he wants to teach the history of Islam on a popular Dutch television channel is a sign of where he thinks his home is. He told me something that sounded sinister, but may actually be the beginning of a solution: "The body of Islam," he said, "is in the Middle East, but the mind is in Europe." Europe provides the freedom to explore, to reform, and to challenge. Olivier Roy, the famous French scholar of Islam, has argued that Islam must be accepted as a European religion.[4] The only chance for a peaceful future is for European Islam to accommodate itself to liberal democracy. Abdelhakim, in his confused, defensive, prickly way, may be groping toward such an accommodation.

The website elqalem.nl, for which he writes, is provocative, sometimes offensive, and often plain wrongheaded, but it is still a forum for debate. There is an attempt to engage with society with words, and not violence. Much of what goes on in the chatrooms of this website, and others like it, such as marokko.nl, revolves around a serious question: how to be a Muslim in a secular European society, how to be a Dutch citizen without losing pride in a separate identity that is so often reviled. Marokko.nl once ran a discussion between young Muslims about anal sex; what did the Koran have to say about this practice? Far from being frivolous, the subject showed precisely the conflict of modern identities.

Young Muslim girls, like most Europeans of their generation, want to have sex with their boyfriends, but still feel the pressure to enter marriage as virgins.

Religion provides rules of behavior. It answers questions of moral right and wrong. It can offer people a sense of pride. The rules may be questionable and the answers open to challenge. But people should be free to work these issues out for themselves. An illiterate villager in the Rif mountains might not have been able to use this freedom. All he or she knew was village custom and the word of God. Educated Europeans, such as Abdelhakim, are better placed to make their own choices. In modern society, religious orthodoxy, though by definition closed to reasonable argument, is often a choice. And as such it should be accepted, as long as the choice is not foisted on others.

Religion can also fuel hatred and become a source of political violence. Amsterdam, like any big city in Europe and beyond, is now linked, through a network of instant communication, to a global revolutionary movement based on an extremist, and largely modern, interpretation of Islam. To join this movement was the choice of Mohammed Bouyeri. Like all forms of political violence, this is indefensible, not only from the perspective of secular law-abiding citizens, but from the perspective of most Muslim believers as well. Revolutionary Islam is linked to the Koran, to be sure, just as Stalinism and Maoism were linked to *Das Kapital*, but to explain the horrors of China's man-made famines or the Soviet gulag solely by invoking the writings of Karl Marx would be to miss the main point. Messianic violence can attach itself to any creed. Abdelhakim is not Mohammed Bouyeri. He, and others like him, could yet choose to join his murderous cause, but such a choice depends partly on the way they are treated by the country in which they were born. And this depends on another choice: whether to accept an orthodox Muslim as a fellow free citizen of a European country.

I boarded the tram to the soccer stadium in Rotterdam, in a rush of orange supporters. Inside the tram, grown men in carnival costumes were jumping up and down with a fervor that blurred the borderlines between ecstasy and fury. I tried to bury my face in the newspaper. Spotting my stand-offishness, one man started bellowing the Dutch national anthem into my ear. When I looked up from my paper, he screamed: "Don't you love Holland?" His face was flushed with what looked to me like rage. I mouthed a somewhat cowardly "sure I do," hoping that he would go away. Others around him were shouting "Germany is finished, Germany is finished!" And then, as an afterthought: "We haven't forgotten the war!"

Rotterdam's magnificent stadium was a sea of orange, waving the national red, white, and blue. I saw one person with the replica of a cow on top of his orange jester's hat. There were banners with the names of supporter groups from various Dutch towns. I saw people in clogs dancing to an old-fashioned brass band. Like all carnivals, this patriotic feast, with shades of a Brueghel painting, was a fantasy, the celebration of an imaginary community, rural, joyous, traditional, and white. It was a return to an invented country, no more real than a modern Dutch Muslim's fantasy of the pure world of the Prophet.

Both fantasies contain the seeds of destruction. The orange men seem relatively harmless. Their patriotism, by and large, is a festive holiday from postwar political pieties. But on November 2, 2004, the violent fantasies of a Dutch Muslim ended in the murder of a fellow citizen. I have described some of the responses to this deed over the course of a year, some sensible, some vicious, some plain silly. But the story is not over. What happened in this small corner of northwestern Europe could happen anywhere, as long as young men and women feel that death is their only way home.

Postscript

In April, 2006, Ayaan Hirsi Ali was informed that she could no longer stay in her apartment on the eleventh floor of a quiet, well-guarded residential building in The Hague. Before moving into that apartment, acquired for her by the Dutch state, she had been passed on from one shelter to another, like a fugitive in an occupied country. Her new neighbors complained that they no longer felt safe with her in the building, and took their complaints to court. They lost in the first instance but won on appeal. Hirsi Ali was given four months to move. She decided to move to the United States.

Her reaction was entirely in the spirit of modern Dutch public discourse. She talked about the war. No wonder, she said with a bitter smile, that the Dutch had failed to stand up to the Nazis: "A terror regime of political correctness is ruling over our country."

A few weeks later, another bombshell. Rita ("Iron Rita") Verdonk, the minister for immigration and integration, had decided that Holland was not even Hirsi Ali's country. It never had been, for Ayaan had lied about her name and provenance when she had applied for asylum. She was not Ayaan Hirsi Ali but Ayaan Hirsi Magan. This cannot have been news to the minister, since Ayaan had said as much to many people, including me. But she repeated it in a television documentary in April, just as "Iron Rita" was running for the leadership of the conservative party, the VVD. The same woman whose handshake was refused by the orthodox imam, the same sturdy symbol of the Dutch confrontation with an alien creed, had now turned on her own colleague.

And so Ayaan Hirsi Ali became the latest victim of a hard line on refugees and immigrants. Holland would no longer be a soft touch. Rita would "keep a straight back." An Iraqi family was sent back home despite warnings of great danger. Terrified refugees had been returned to Syria and Congo together with their personal files, which would lead to further persecution. Others were locked up in prison cells after their shelter at the Amsterdam airport went up in flames and eleven people died. A schoolgirl from Kosovo was more or less dragged out of her school just before completing her exams. The midnight knock on the door was becoming a real threat in a society that was proud of its tolerance.

This was never what Ayaan had wanted. She was neither a xenophobe nor opposed to immigrants (how could she be?). But she had called the Dutch cowards, like those people during the war who looked away while their neighbors were being deported. She had lamented their weakness in not standing up to the Islamist threat. She and Rita Verdonk were allies. Verdonk, a former deputy prison warden, simply lacked the subtlety or the imagination to draw a clear line between getting tough on political Islam and on refugees who fell foul of petty bureaucratic rules.

Hirsi Ali will not be sent back to Somalia, or even Kenya. The minister's treatment of her colleague caused such an uproar that Ayaan's citizenship is probably safe. But it was a melancholy end to an extraordinary odyssey that started with a white lie to escape an arranged marriage. No one in the last few hundred years has managed to stir up so much in the Netherlands as this "bogus asylum seeker." She could not stand the liberal platitudes and anxious consensus-building that obscured what she saw as a lethal threat to civil liberties. So she went to war, dogmatically perhaps, a little zealously even, but always armed with nothing but her own convictions. It resulted in a lethal battle, fought first with words and then with bullets and knives. Theo van Gogh is dead. Mohammed Bouyeri is locked up in prison alone with the words of his holy books. And Ayaan Hirsi Ali has had to leave the scene. My country seems smaller without her.

Acknowledgments

Without Avishai Margalit's encouragement I might never have written this book. My extended stay in Amsterdam was made possible by the unstinting hospitality of Hanca Leppink and Hans Baaij, and the generosity of Heikelien Verijn Stuart and Stan van Houcke, who gave me the run of their wonderful house.

Many people helped me in my research, by providing contacts, insights, and stimulation, or simply by making time to be interviewed. I shall list those to whom I feel particularly grateful in alphabetical order: Ahmed Aboutaleb, Samir Bantal, Jan Blokker, Hans Blom, Ybo Buruma, Nora Choua, Abdelhakim Chouaati, Job Cohen, Willem Diepraam, Egbert Dommering, Jan Donkers, Ali Eddaoudi, Afshin Ellian, Emile Fallaux, Nico Frijda, Janny Groen, Sadik Harchaoui, Judith Herzberg, Ayaan Hirsi Ali, Theodor Holman, Harko Keyzer, Shamanee Kempadoo, Margalith Kleiwegt, Geert Mak, Fouad Mourigh, Funda Müjde, Max Pam, Herman Philipse, Els van der Plas, Bellari Said, Paul Scheffer, R. V. Schipper, Bart Jan Spruyt, Abram de Swaan, Dubravka Ugresic, Gijs van de Westelaken, and Jolande Withuis.

I owe thanks to two more people who agreed to be interviewed. It was an animated discussion about a sensitive topic. A mistake has been pointed out in the attribution, but every word has been accurately conveyed. Due to the delicate nature of the comments, I have opted to use initials which do not corespond to their real names.

I also owe a great debt to three members of a sadly diminishing breed, publishers who are also great editors: Emile Brugman, Scott

Moyers, and Toby Mundy. Any mistakes in the book are my responsibility alone. Thanks, too, to Jin Auh of the Wylie Agency in New York. And finally, to Eri Hotta, my wife, the value of whose support and encouragement cannot be adequately expressed in words.

Notes

Chapter 2: Thank You, Pim

1. Nova, September 29, 2004.
2. *Trouw,* April 17, 1999.
3. *Volkskrant,* February 9, 2002.
4. Quoted in Dick Pels, *De geest van Pim* (Anthos, 2003), p. 63.
5. *Lof van het conservatisme* (Balans, 2003).
6. I owe a debt for this analysis to Dick Pels's book on Fortuyn.
7. Pels, p. 201.
8. Ibid., p. 66.

Chapter 3: The Healthy Smoker

1. *HP/De Tijd,* November 12, 2004.
2. *De Gezonde Roker,* December 21, 2003.

Chapter 4: A Dutch Tragedy

1. *Metro,* November 3, 2004.
2. *Trouw,* May 26, 2004.

Chapter 5: Submission

1. Jutta Chorus and Ahmet Olgun, *In godsnaam* (Contact: Amsterdam, 2005).

2. *De maagdenkooi* (Augustus: Amsterdam, 2004).

3. *Volkskrant,* August 18, 2005.

4. This story, and much of the above, was recounted in Ayaan Hirsi Ali's *De zoontjesfabriek* (Augustus: Amsterdam, 2002).

5. Ibid., p. 16.

6. *De maagdenkooi,* p. 20.

7. *Submission* (Augustus: Amsterdam, 2004).

Chapter 6: A Promising Boy

1. *De ideologische en religieuze ontwikkeling van Mohammed Bouyeri. Rapport van het deskundigenonderzoek in de strafzaak tegen M. Bouyeri,* Prof. Dr. Mr. Ruud Peters.

2. *NRC Handelsblad,* July 9, 2005.

3. Much of this information is from a report by Jaco Alberts, Jutta Chorus, Steven Derix, and Ahmet Olgun published in *NRC Handelsblad,* July 9, 2005.

4. *Trouw,* July 9, 2005.

5. This and other anecdotes are recounted by Jutta Chorus and Ahmet Olgun in their book *In godsnaam: Het jaar van Theo van Gogh* (Amsterdam, 2005).

6. Quoted in the Peters report.

7. Open Letter to the Dutch People, August 12, 2004.

8. Bas Heijne, *Hollandse toestande* (Prometheus, 2005).

Chapter 7: In Memoriam

1. *Het Parool,* October 12, 2005.

2. November 4, 2004.

3. Elsevier.nl, December 8, 2005.

4. See his *Failure of Political Islam.*

Index

Islam as threat to, 193, 210, 245, 246

Der Spiegel, 140n

Deyssel, Lodewijk van, 97

DHC, 141, 142, 143

Diana, princess of Wales, 65

Dijkstal, Hans, 59

Dirty Paper, The (Van Gogh), 72

dish cities, 21, 54–55, 110, 149–51, 159–60, 162

Disraeli, Benjamin, 61

Dittrich, Boris, 99, 100

Douar Ikhammalen, 196–97

Downfall, The (Presser), 81

Dutch East Indies, 12–13, 19, 80

Dutch society

  character of, 10–12, 15, 26, 35, 41, 50, 154–55, 161, 203, 221, 230–31, 238

  demographic changes in, 118–19

  history curriculum in, 255, 256

  immigration to. *See* immigrants and immigration

  Islam and, 4–8, 17–18, 25, 51, 53, 108, 128, 139–40, 234

  as moral beacon, 217

  pillars of, 48, 245

  postwar generation, 19, 51, 83

  progressivism of, 11–12

  religious freedom in, 18

Eddaoudi, Ali, 204–5, 214–16, 221

Ede, 159–60, 162

Elias, Norbert, 167

Ellian, Afshin, 24–25, 31, 155–58, 166

elqalem.nl, 249, 259

Enlightenment, 18–19, 25, 27, 28–29, 31–35, 169, 191–92

  Hirsi Ali on, 167–68

Enzensberger, Hans Magnus, 140n

Erasmus, Desiderius, 192

Eternal Jew, The, 240

European-Arab League, 99, 120

European Cup, 254

European Union, 29, 67, 174

European unity, 50

Fahmi (Bouyeri's friend), 223

Fatwas on Women (Ibn Taymiyah), 252

February Strike, 85, 237–38

female circumcision, 146

Feyenoord, 43, 84, 85

Fortuyn, Pim, 6, 39, 220

  bitterness of, 62

  childhood of, 60

  followers of, 62–63, 66–69

  funeral of, 42–44, 64–65

  as greatest Dutch figure, 45

  homosexuality of, 39, 54, 55–56, 57, 60, 62

  house of, 61

  immigration, views on, 46, 67

  Islam and, 56–57

  on leadership, 67–68

  manner and appearance of, 58–59

  murder of, 37, 39–40, 39–41, 220

  political background of, 56

  political career of, 45–46, 59

  statue of, 45

  Van Gogh and, 39, 69–70, 93

  writings of, 58

Forum, 108–9, 204, 247

France, EU and, 67, 174

Frank, Anne, 19, 45, 51–52, 83, 231–32, 240

freedom of speech, 137, 148

Friendly Conversation, A, 9

Friends of Theo, 9, 14–15, 16, 94, 109, 191, 227, 230, 238